Exellen

THE

QUOTABLE
LAWYER

THE

QUOTABLE
LAWYER

Edited by Tony Lyons

Skyhorse Publishing

Skyhorse Publishing books may be purchased in bulk at special discounts for sales promotion, corporate gifts, fund-raising, or educational purposes. Special editions can also be created to specifications. For details, contact the Special Sales Department, Skyhorse Publishing, 555 Eighth Avenue, Suite 903, New York, NY 10018 or info@skyhorsepublishing.com.

www.skyhorsepublishing.com

10 9 8 7 6 5 4 3 2 1

Library of Congress Cataloging-in-Publication Data

The quotable lawyer / edited and introduced by Tony Lyons.
    p. cm.
 Includes index.
 ISBN 978-1-60239-947-1 (alk. paper)
 1. Law--Quotations. I. Lyons, Tony.
 K58.Q678 2010
 340--dc22

                          2009039538

Printed in China

Acknowledgments

For my ex-wife, Helena, against whom I would need a very special lawyer in order to win an argument.

Thanks to my brother Charlie for helping with the censorship section; to my brother Paul for helping with the introduction, the literary quotes, and the organization; and to my father, Nick, for his comments and encouragement.

Contents

Introduction		*ix*
1	Some Premises of the Law	1
2	Society, the Individual, and the Law	15
3	The Machinery of the Law	55
4	The Practice of Law	101
5	Law, Money, and Power	143
6	Justice and Injustice	167
7	Cases and Judgments	227
8	Freedom and Censorship	249
9	Crime and Punishment	285
10	At the Expense of Lawyers:	
	Quips, Jokes, and Scandalous Sayings	311
Contributors		345
Works Cited		359
Author Index		373

Introduction

Society can never take its laws for granted. The law is a quest for justice—sometimes that quest edges closer, sometimes it drifts away—but the results are always a combination of time-honored precedent and the efforts of individuals. As United States Supreme Court Justice Oliver Wendell Holmes, Jr. wrote:

> The law embodies a story of a nation's development through many centuries, and it cannot be dealt with as if it contained only the axioms and corollaries of a book of mathematics.

That development is a series of dramas with uncertain outcomes. Individuals and groups throughout society play a central role in the legal process by voting for political candidates who promise to pass certain laws, or by lobbying or protesting to influence the laws passed by the legislative branch of government. The law changes because of societal pressure, and society changes because of the law. The judicial branch interprets those laws, deciding whether or not they are consistent with the Constitution. It then fashions remedies to ensure that reality approximates the law and hands down decisions to deter or punish wrongful conduct. At the heart of these dramas are thousands of lawyers arguing to have one interpretation of the law or the facts triumph over another. The lawyer is both mechanic and architect.

We live in an incredibly litigious society in which anyone can sue anyone about anything. At the center of the mayhem, lawyers are at once distrusted, feared, and romanticized. They are known for their eloquence and persuasion—for reaching into a bag of rhetorical tricks that have the potential to manipulate. Lawyers frequently are on the receiving end of unflattering humor and disdain, but at the same time they are often portrayed as heroes in some of the most highly rated TV shows, most successful movies, and best-selling novels. In these stories, lawyers are often cast as advocates for the downtrodden against tobacco or insurance companies or the criminal justice system. But they are also portrayed as the least trustworthy members of society—ambulance chasers, mob lawyers, even devil's advocates. The media respond to the American public's fascination with lawyers at the same time that these polarized portrayals add to the mystique.

Underlying this fascination with lawyers is the sense that a society is characterized by its laws—the actions that it allows or even encourages, and those that it chooses to criminalize and punish. The law is a kind of nervous system for society. In the trials of individuals such as Socrates, Joan of Arc, Dreyfus, Antigone, O.J. Simpson, suspected terrorists, or even Bill Clinton, as well as in landmark cases such as *Nixon v. U.S., Bush v. Gore, Brown v. Board of Education,* or the recent scandals involving companies such as

Enron or WorldCom, society itself is on trial, and the law becomes a way in which society talks to itself about what it has become, what it wants to avoid, and the possibilities for the future.

The suspicion of lawyers arises from a deep-seated fear of being at the mercy of the law. Throughout history, people have been imprisoned or even executed for acts of which they were either innocent, or which would have been legal had they been committed in another place and time. Consider the trial of Galileo, the Salem witch trials, the McCarthy hearings, the protracted imprisonment of Nelson Mandela, and hundreds or even thousands of other cases involving world leaders, homeless people, and everyone in between. At the same time, certain individuals have thrived, even been revered as pillars of society, while enslaving their fellow human beings, looting other countries, polluting the environment, committing sex offenses, engaging in insider trading, or committing other heinous acts. As Martin Luther King, Jr. wrote:

> We should never forget that everything Hitler did in Germany was legal and everything the Hungarian freedom fighters did in Hungary was illegal.

Whether an individual is a hero or a criminal is often a question of timing—and obedience to the laws of one regime might be a crime against humanity for another. Most people follow the current law most of the time, and they ought to. This adherence to societal norms creates the confidence that makes possible a productive and orderly society. But some things are simply wrong, whether they are laws, actions taken in blind obedience to those laws, or efforts made to twist the laws, usually for money or power. Somewhere deep down we all know where the line is. As Herman Melville wrote in *Typee*:

> The grand principles of virtue and honor, however they may be distorted by arbitrary codes, are the same all the world over: and where these principles are concerned, the right or wrong of any action appears to be the same to the uncultivated as to the enlightened mind.

No law or fame or material success can protect you against that universal truth. "History," Joseph Schumpeter writes, "consists of a series of short-run situations that may alter the course of events for good." There is no guarantee that truth and justice will triumph over falsehood and persecution, but lawyers, more than anyone else, have the power to plead that they should. By following the logical conclusions of an actively functioning conscience, lawyers can make the world a less volatile and more humane place. To the extent that a lawyer is someone who fights for justice, we all practice law in some form or another at some point in our lives.

The quotations collected here touch on a broad range of concepts, often only loosely related to law or lawyers. I broadened the definitions of each to include the concepts of justice and freedom, and the effects of power and money on their execution. I included the legal system and the lawyers who operate within it, as well as those operating outside of the system—philosophers, politicians, or preachers—who act as lawyers in the court of public opinion. All divisions are arbitrary, and there is certainly a degree of overlap, but I divided the quotations into sections to create an orderly presentation and some sense of a narrative essay.

The first chapter offers some premises upon which laws are or should be based; the second includes quotations about the interactions among society, the individual, and the law—how law functions to solidify society and the range of benefits and consequences. Chapters 3 and 4 deal with the machinery and practice of law—how the system works and how lawyers operate within it. Chapter 5 explores the powerful sway money and power often exercise over the legal process. This leads naturally to the questions of justice and injustice raised in Chapter 6. Chapter 7 includes quotations from or about specific cases and the judgments rendered, while Chapter 8 addresses our constitutional liberties and efforts, especially censorship, to restrict those freedoms. Chapter 9 looks at what happens when individual actions exceed individual rights and those accused of crimes are tried and, if found guilty, punished.

Being entangled in the legal system, as most people are at some point, engenders a cluster of emotions—anxiety, frustration, fear, anger, hope, and sometimes, when the settlements are high, euphoria. Since humor often becomes a way of processing these kinds of emotions as well as a form of acceptance, it is no surprise that there are more jokes about lawyers than about any other professionals. The final chapter takes a glimpse at the variety of ways in which people have poked fun at lawyers and their profession.

I hope you enjoy reading these quotations as much as I enjoyed gathering them.

–Tony Lyons

1

Some Premises
of the Law

The continued existence of a free and democratic society depends upon the recognition of the concept that justice is based upon the rule of law grounded in respect for the dignity of the individual and the capacity of the individual, through reason, for enlightened self-government. Law so grounded makes justice possible, for only through such law does the dignity of the individual attain respect and protection. Without it, individual rights become subject to unrestrained power, respect for law is destroyed, and rational self-government is impossible.

THE NEW YORK STATE BAR ASSOCIATION
The Lawyer's Code of Professional Responsibility (1999)

The law is the witness and external deposit of our moral life. Its history is the history of the moral development of the race.

U.S. SUPREME COURT JUSTICE OLIVER WENDELL HOLMES, JR.
SPEECH IN BOSTON (JANUARY 8, 1897)

We should never forget that everything Hitler did in Germany was legal and everything the Hungarian freedom fighters did in Hungary was illegal.

MARTIN LUTHER KING, JR.
Letter from Birmingham Jail (1963)

A system of justice is the richer for diversity of background and experience. It is the poorer, in terms of appreciating what is at stake and the impact of its judgments, if its members—its lawyers, jurors, and judges—are all cast from the same mold.

U.S. SUPREME COURT JUSTICE RUTH BADER GINSBURG,
SPEECH GIVEN AT WELLESLEY COLLEGE (NOVEMBER 13, 1998)

Laws and institutions must go hand in hand with the progress of the human mind.

PRESIDENT THOMAS JEFFERSON (1743–1826)

The spirit of the law is true necessity, which compels man into the social state, now and always, by a still-beginning, never-ceasing force of moral cohesion.

RUFUS CHOATE (1799–1859)
CITING SAMUEL TAYLOR COLERIDGE (1772–1834)

The life of the law has not been logic; it has been experience.

U.S. SUPREME COURT JUSTICE OLIVER WENDELL HOLMES, JR.
(1841–1935)

No man is above the law and no man is below it; nor do we ask any man's permission when we ask him to obey it.

PRESIDENT THEODORE ROOSEVELT (1858–1919)

Good laws lead to the making of better ones; bad ones bring about worse.

JEAN JACQUES ROUSSEAU
The Social Contract (1762)

The notion of the regulation and reconciliation of conflicts through rule by law—and the elaboration of rules and procedures which, on occasion, made some approximate approach towards the ideal—seems to me . . . a cultural achievement of universal significance.

E. P. THOMPSON (1924–1993)

Ye shall have one manner of law, as well for the stranger, as for one of your own country.

LEVITICUS 24:22

Equal justice under law is not just a caption on the facade of the Supreme Court building. It is perhaps the most inspiring ideal of our society . . . It is fundamental that justice should be the same, in substance and availability, without regard to economic status.

U.S. SUPREME COURT JUSTICE LEWIS POWELL, JR. (1907–)

Whatever disagreement there may be as to the scope of the phrase "due process of law" there can be no doubt that it embraces the fundamental conception of a fair trial, with opportunity to be heard.

U.S. SUPREME COURT JUSTICE OLIVER WENDELL HOLMES, JR.
Frank v. Mangum (1915)

To no one will we sell, to no one will we refuse or delay, right or justice.

Magna Carta (1215)

———

The law is a spider's web: the bumblebee will tear it to shreds, but the midge will get stuck.

OLD RUSSIAN PROVERB

Where laws end, tyranny begins.

WILLIAM PITT (1759–1806)

———

Self-preservation is the very law of life. Affirmation of existence, the will to live, is written in the constitution of all living things.

PHILIP H. PHENIX
Man and His Becoming (1964)

Truth is never pure, rarely simple.

OSCAR WILDE (1854–1900)

It is the spirit and not the form of law that keeps justice alive.

U.S. CHIEF JUSTICE EARL WARREN (1891–1974)

Let reverence for the laws . . . become the political religion of the nation.

PRESIDENT ABRAHAM LINCOLN (1809–1865)

What a subject is . . . this abstraction called the Law, wherein, as in a magic mirror, we see reflected, not only our own lives, but the lives of all the men that have been.

U.S. SUPREME COURT JUSTICE OLIVER WENDELL HOLMES, JR.
The Common Law (1881)

There is no one who can adequately explain what your reactions ought to be when your client is absolutely guilty or has the weaker case, or how to conduct yourself and still present a substantial position for your client when the money simply is not there, the time is short, the spirit is weak, the witness uncooperative, and you have a family or other personal matters competing for your time.

ROBERT GOLDMAN
The Modern Art of Cross-Examination (1993)

The law may be rhetoric, but it need not be empty rhetoric.

E. P. THOMPSON (1924–1993)

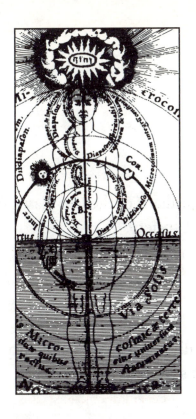

2

Society, the Individual, and the Law

Lawyers, as guardians of the law, play a vital role in the preservation of society.

THE NEW YORK STATE BAR ASSOCIATION
The Lawyer's Code of Professional Responsibility (1999)

It is emphatically the province and duty of the judicial department to say what the law is.

U.S. SUPREME COURT JUSTICE JOHN MARSHALL (1755–1835)

What, then, has become of that part of the constitution which declares ours to be a government of laws, and not of men?

ATTORNEY GENERAL SULLIVAN (1928)

A government of laws, and not of men.

PRESIDENT JOHN ADAMS (1735–1826)

Lack of confidence kills a civilization. We can destroy ourselves by cynicism and disillusion just as effectively as by bombs.

KENNETH CLARK
Civilization (1970)

There are only two types of governments: those that can maintain order and those that cannot.

SAMUEL P. HUNTINGTON
American Politics: The Promise of Disharmony (1983)

Leaving things to the government, like leaving them to providence, is synonymous with not caring about them.

JOHN STUART MILL
Utilitarianism, Liberty, and Representative Government
(1859)

The harsh truth is that we may well be on our way to a society overrun by hordes of lawyers, hungry as locusts, and brigades of judges in numbers never before contemplated.

U.S. CHIEF JUSTICE WARREN BURGER (1907–1995)

The virtuous need but few laws; for it is not the law which determines their actions, but their actions which determine the law.

THEOPHRASTUS (372–286 B.C.)

Loyalty to the principles upon which our Government rests positively demands that the equality before the law which it guarantees to every citizen should be justly and in good faith conceded in all parts of the land

PRESIDENT GROVER CLEVELAND
SECOND INAUGURAL ADDRESS (MARCH 4, 1893)

Any man who seeks to deny equality among all his brothers betrays the spirit of the free and invites the mockery of the tyrant.

PRESIDENT DWIGHT D. EISENHOWER
INAUGURAL ADDRESS (1953)

All, too, will bear in mind this sacred principle, that though the will of the majority is in all cases to prevail, that will to be rightful must be reasonable; that the minority possess their equal rights, which equal law must protect, and to violate would be oppression.

PRESIDENT THOMAS JEFFERSON
FIRST INAUGURAL ADDRESS (MARCH 4, 1801)

Lawyers must be activists to leave a contribution to society. The law is more than a control; it is an instrument for social change.

E. CLINTON BAMBERGER, DIRECTOR OF THE OFFICE OF EQUAL OPPORTUNITY'S LEGAL SERVICES PROGRAM, IN A SPEECH TO THE NATIONAL LEGAL AID AND DEFENDER ASSOCIATION (NOVEMBER 18, 1965)

The liberties of none are safe unless the liberties of all are protected.

U.S. CHIEF JUSTICE WILLIAM O. DOUGLAS (1898–1980)

The law does not pretend to punish everything that is dishonest. That would seriously interfere with business.

CLARENCE DARROW (1857–1938)

Lawyers are necessary in a community. Some of you . . . take a different view; but as I am a member of that legal profession, or was at one time, and have only lost standing in it to become a politician, I still retain the pride of the profession. And I still insist that it is the law and the lawyer that make popular government under a written constitution and written statutes possible.

PRESIDENT WILLIAM HOWARD TAFT (1857–1930)

. . . the Department of Justice is committed to asking one central question of everything we do: What is the right thing to do? Now that can produce debate, and I want it to be spirited debate. I want the lawyers of America to be able to call me and tell me: Janet, have you lost your mind?

U.S. ATTORNEY GENERAL JANET RENO,

QUOTED IN *The New York Times Magazine* (MAY 15, 1994)

That great law of nature: self-preservation.

Samuel Butler (1835–1902)

If what is important about law is that it functions to "legitimate" the existing order, one starts to ask how it does that.

Robert Gorden (1871)

He was at a loss how it should come to pass, that the law which was intended for every man's preservation, should be any man's ruin . . . ; he thought nature and reason were sufficient guides for a reasonable animal, as we pretended to be, in showing us what we ought to do, and what to avoid.

JONATHAN SWIFT
Gulliver's Travels (1726)

The trick is not to ignore self-interest but to redefine it, to make it less myopic and more empathic.

EDWARD WEISBAND
Poverty Amidst Plenty (1989)

But if there is an attitude that society is gaining by eradicating poverty, if there is a positive attempt to bring these millions of the poor to the point where they can make their contribution to the United States, that will make a huge difference. The spirit of a campaign against poverty does not cost a single cent. It is a matter of vision.

MICHAEL HARRINGTON
The Other America: Poverty in the United States (1962)

The error of free market economics is that it substitutes an automatic social mechanism for moral responsibility and thereby permits grave social injustice to occur.

PHILIP H. PHENIX
Man and His Becoming (1964)

No government can exist without some measure of hierarchy, inequality, arbitrary power, secrecy, deception, and established patterns of subordination and superordination.

SAMUEL HUNTINGTON
American Politics: The Promise of Disharmony (1983)

There is no grievance that is a fit object of redress by mob rule.

PRESIDENT ABRAHAM LINCOLN (1809–1865)

However chaotic and uncertain modern life might appear, we still live by the Rule of Law.

ROBERT TRAVER
The Jealous Mistress (1967)

The law is simply and solely made for the exploitation of those who do not understand it or of those who, for naked need, cannot obey it.

BERTOLT BRECHT
The Threepenny Opera (1928)

The less government we have, the better—the fewer laws, and the less confided power.

RALPH WALDO EMERSON (1803–1882)

We may lament, then, the errors of the times, which led to these persecutions. But surely our ancestors had no special reasons for shame in a belief, which had the universal sanction of their own and all former ages; which counted in its train philosophers . . . which the law supported by its mandates, and the purest of judges felt no compunctions in enforcing.

JOSEPH STORY (1828)

Moralism ensures that government will never truly be efficacious; the realities of power ensure that government will never truly be democratic.

SAMUEL HUNTINGTON
American Politics: The Promise of Disharmony (1983)

Fragile as reason is and limited as law is as the institutionalized medium of reason, that's all we have standing between us and the tyranny of mere will and the cruelty of unbridled, undisciplined feeling.

U.S. SUPREME COURT JUSTICE FELIX FRANKFURTER
Felix Frankfurter Reminisces (1960)

Those who are too lazy and comfortable to think for themselves and be their own judges obey the laws. Others sense their own laws within them.

HERMANN HESSE
Demian (1919)

We live in perilous times, in which our fair and splendid fabrics of Governments, and our wide and deep jurisprudence, are threatened to be weakened and disturbed to their very foundations. May you . . . prove a stable and impregnable bulwark against all dangerous innovation, and all ferocious assault, of the splendid structures created by the wisdom and patriotism of our fathers.

CHANCELLOR JAMES KENT, IN A LETTER TO JOSEPH STORY (1833)

If you will accept bold ideas, new theories, courageous innovation, and disputed principles with an open and inquisitive mind and a renewed commitment to make the law an instrument of advantage for disadvantaged people, we will be a significant generation.

E. CLINTON BAMBERGER, FIRST DIRECTOR OF THE OEO LEGAL SERVICES PROGRAM, IN A SPEECH TO THE NATIONAL LEGAL AID AND DEFENDER ASSOCIATION (NOVEMBER 18, 1965)

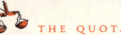

As lawyers, our first responsibility is, of course, to see that the legal profession provides adequate representation for all people in our society. I would suggest there is no subject which is more important to the legal profession, that is more important to this nation, than . . . the realization of the ideal of equal justice under law for all.

RICHARD NIXON, IN HIS SPEECH TO THE NATIONAL LEGAL AID AND DEFENDER ASSOCIATION (OCTOBER 1962)

[E]very one of us is responsible for everyone else in every way ... everyone is really responsible for everyone and everything ...

FATHER ZOSSIMA, NARRATING A CONVERSATION BETWEEN HIS
YOUNGER BROTHER AND HIS MOTHER; FYODOR DOSTOYEVSKY,
The Brothers Karamazov (1879)

We all have power—the capacity to influence, alter, affect the lives of those around us.

MARILYN FRENCH
Beyond Power: On Women, Men and Morals (1986)

We can't stir a finger in this world without the risk of bringing death to somebody . . . ; once I'd definitely refused to kill, I doomed myself to an exile that can never end.

> ALBERT CAMUS
> *The Plague* (1957)

Everything kills everything in some way.

> ERNEST HEMINGWAY
> *The Old Man and the Sea* (1952)

People who make too many altruistic demands on themselves may after a time lose the inclination to go on doing good works, with the result that over the course of their lives they do less good than they would have done by starting at a sustainable rate.

JONATHAN GLOVER
Causing Death and Saving Lives (1977)

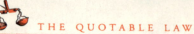

Once the door is opened to calculations of utility and national interest, the usual speculations about the future of freedom, peace, and economic prosperity can be brought to bear to ease the consciences of those responsible for a certain number of charred babies.

THOMAS NAGEL

"WAR AND MASSACRE" (2002)

It is in the Koran, not the New Testament, that we read the maxim: A ruler who appoints any man to an office, when there is in his dominions another man better qualified for it, sins against God and against the State.

JOHN STUART MILL
On Liberty (1859)

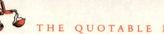
A presidential election is sometimes ... a turning point in history.

JAMES BRYCE (1888)

You can fool some of the people some of the time, but you can never fool all of the people all of the time.

PRESIDENT THOMAS JEFFERSON (1743–1826)

History, however, consists of a succession of short-run situations that may alter the course of events for good. If all the people can in the short run be "fooled" step by step into something they do not really want, and if this is not an exceptional case which we could afford to neglect, then no amount of retrospective common sense will alter the fact that in reality they neither raise nor decide issues but that the issues that shape their fate are normally raised and decided for them.

JOSEPH A. SCHUMPETER
Capitalism, Socialism and Democracy (1942)

The mistakes committed by ignorance in a virtuous disposition would never be of such fatal consequence to the public weal, as the practices of a man whose inclinations led him to be corrupt, and had great abilities to manage, and multiply, and defend his corruptions.

JONATHAN SWIFT
Gulliver's Travels (1726)

[Democratic nations] cover the whole of social life with a network of petty, complicated rules that are both minute and uniform, through which even men of the greatest originality and the most vigorous temperament cannot force their head above the crowd. It does not break men's will, but softens, bends, and guides it; it seldom enjoins, but often inhibits, action; it does not destroy anything, but prevents much from being born; it is not at all tyrannical, but it hinders, restrains, enervates, stifles, and stultifies so much that in the end each nation is no more than a flock of timid and hardworking animals with the government as its shepherd.

ALEXIS DE TOCQUEVILLE
Democracy in America (1835)

We felt often that we were perceived as mothers trying to be lawyers, while a male colleague of ours who had a young child was perceived as a lawyer who also happened to be a father.

ATTORNEYS ANNE C. WEISBERG AND CAROL A. BUCKLER
Everything a Working Mother Needs to Know (1994)

If equity and human natural reason were allowed there would be no law, there would be no lawyers.

CHRISTINA STEAD, AUSTRALIAN NOVELIST,
QUOTED IN *House of All Nations (1938)*

It could probably be shown by facts and figures that there is no distinctly native American criminal class except Congress.

MARK TWAIN (1835–1910)

To find citizens ruled by good and wholesome laws, that is an exceedingly rare and hard thing.

SIR THOMAS MORE (1478–1535)

The founders of a new colony, whatever Utopia of human virtue and happiness they might originally project, have invariably recognized it as among their earliest practical necessities to allot a portion of the virgin soil as a cemetery, and another portion as the site of a prison.

NATHANIEL HAWTHORNE
The Scarlet Letter (1850)

A bad law should be corrected only by legislative action, but so long as it remains in force, it is to be respected as law, and because it is law, not grudgingly and reluctantly, but with honesty and sincerity, because any departure from the fundamental rule of conduct would put in jeopardy every interest and every institution which is worth saving.

MASSACHUSETTS SUPREME COURT CHIEF JUSTICE LEMUEL SHAW (1781–1861)

The duty, in case of shipwreck, of a captain to his crew, of the crew to the passengers, of soldiers to women and children . . . is to impose on men the moral necessity, not of the preservation, but of the sacrifice of their lives for others, from which in no country, least of all, it is to be hoped, in England, will men ever shrink, as indeed, they have not shrunk.

LORD COLERIDGE, JUDGMENT ON *R. v. Dudley and Stephens* INVOLVING CANNIBALISM AT SEA (1884)

One law for the Lion and the Ox is oppression.

WILLIAM BLAKE
"THE MARRIAGE OF HEAVEN AND HELL" (1794)

Society, as constituted, is truly a world turned upside down . . . with regard to morality, the most immoral are expected to train citizens in virtue; and with regard to administrative justice, the big crooks are chosen to punish the faults of the petty delinquents.

CLAUDE-HENRI DE ROUVROY (1819)

Yet law-abiding scholars write:
Law is neither wrong nor right,
Law is only crimes
Punished by places and times.

W. H. AUDEN
"LAW LIKE LOVE" (1939)

And hard by Temple Bar, in Lincoln's Inn Hall, at the very heart of the fog, sits the Lord High Chancellor in his High Court of Chancery.

CHARLES DICKENS
Bleak House (1853)

With laws shall our land be built up but with lawlessness laid waste.

NJAL'S SAGA (ICELANDIC) (N.D.)

They who can give up essential liberty to obtain a little temporary safety deserve neither liberty nor safety.

BENJAMIN FRANKLIN (1706–1790)

Litigation today means that diplomacy has failed and war has been declared.

ROBERT GOLDMAN
The Modern Art of Cross-Examination (1993)

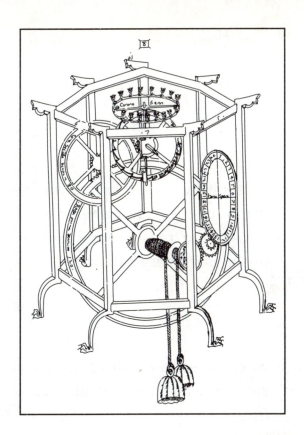

3

The Machinery of the Law

A lawyer's relationship to justice and wisdom is on a par with a piano tuner's relationship to a concert. He neither composes the music, nor interprets it—he merely keeps the machinery running.

LUCILLE KALLEN (1922–1999)

The law is what it is—a majestic edifice, sheltering all of us, each stone of which rests on another.

JOHN GALSWORTHY
Justice (1910)

Laws too gentle are seldom obeyed; too severe, seldom executed.

BENJAMIN FRANKLIN (1706–1790)

———

Through the centuries, men of law have been persistently concerned with the resolution of disputes . . . in ways that enable society to achieve its goals with a minimum of force and maximum of reason.

ARCHIBALD COX (1912–)
PROFESSOR OF LAW, HARVARD LAW SCHOOL

The law, like poetry, is the final resort of the lame, the halt, the imbecile, and the blind. I dare say Caesar invented the law business to protect himself against poets.

WILLIAM FAULKNER
Sartoris (1929)

Never, never, never, on cross-examination ask a witness a question you don't already know the answer to, was a tenet I absorbed with my baby-food. Do it, and you'll often get an answer you don't want, an answer that might wreck your case.

HARPER LEE
To Kill a Mockingbird (1960)

To fight a case on emotional grounds, Miss Winslow, is the surest way of losing it. Emotions muddy the issue. Cold, clear logic—and buckets of it—should be the lawyer's only equipment.

TERENCE RATTIGAN
The Winslow Boy (1946)

Judges, like most people, may be divided roughly into four classes: judges with neither head nor heart—they are to be avoided at all costs; judges with head but no heart—they are almost as bad; then judges with heart but no head—risky but better than the first two, and finally, those rare judges who possess both head and a heart.

ROBERT TRAVER
Anatomy of a Murder (1958)

The legal process, because of its unbridled growth, has become a cancer which threatens the vitality of our forms of capitalism and democracy.

U.S. ATTORNEY GENERAL LAWRENCE SILBERMAN (1935–)

An active trial lawyer must consider everything, which includes not only the case, the personality of his client, his own character traits, and even . . . the weather.

ROBERT GOLDMAN
The Modern Art of Cross-Examination (1993)

All sorts of substitutes for wisdom are used by the world. When the court doesn't know, they use precedent. The court that made the precedent guessed at it. Yesterday's guess, grown gray and wearing a big wig becomes today's justice.

DR. FRANK CRANE (1861–1928)

A lawyer for the defense clears his throat and holds himself ready if the word is "Guilty" to enter a motion for a new trial, speaking in a soft voice, speaking in a voice slightly colored with bitter wrongs mingled with monumental patience, speaking with mythic Atlas shoulders of many preposterous, unjust circumstances.

CARL SANDBURG (1878–1967)

Lawyers are the only persons for whom ignorance of the law is not punished.

JEREMY BENTHAM (1748–1832)

Discourage litigation. Persuade your neighbors to compromise whenever you can. Point out to them how the nominal winner is often a real loser—in fees, expenses, and waste of time. As a peacemaker the lawyer has a superior opportunity of being a good man. There will still be business enough.

PRESIDENT ABRAHAM LINCOLN (1809–1865)

People are intuitively interested in settlement and intuitively repulsed by the complexity and expense associated with our most formal procedures. I'm convinced there's a tremendous appetite for a way other than the win and loss of a court or tribunal decision.

GEORGE ADAMS, FORMER ONTARIO GENERAL COURT DIVISION JUDGE

The eager desire of young practitioners to take part in the exciting contests of the bar; the opportunity afforded to the ambitious to achieve reputation by a display of forensic talent; and the higher motives supplied by feelings of humanity and benevolence will, as we believe, in every case, secure a prompt response to the appointment of the court where the gratuitous services of an attorney are called for.

INDIANA SUPREME COURT
Board of Commissioners v. Pollard (1899)

Reason and reflection require us to recognize that in our adversary system of criminal justice, any person haled into court, who is too poor to hire a lawyer, cannot be assured a fair trial unless counsel is provided for him. This seems to us to be an obvious truth.

U.S. SUPREME COURT JUSTICE HUGO BLACK
Gideon v. Wainwright (1963)

To force a lawyer on a defendant can only lead him to believe that the law contrives against him.

U.S. SUPREME COURT JUSTICE POTTER STEWART (1915–1985)

Litigation should be a last resort, not a knee-jerk reflex.

IRVING S. SHAPIRO (1916–2001)

Do not put such unlimited power into the hands of the husbands.

—ABIGAIL ADAMS (1744–1818)

No living orator would convince a grocer that coffee should be sold without chicory; and no amount of eloquence will make an English lawyer think that loyalty to truth should come before loyalty to his client.

ANTHONY TROLLOPE (1815–1882)

It was a pity . . . that creatures endowed with such prodigious abilities of mind as these lawyers, were not rather encouraged to be instructors of others in wisdom and knowledge.

JONATHAN SWIFT
Gulliver's Travels (1726)

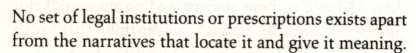

No set of legal institutions or prescriptions exists apart from the narratives that locate it and give it meaning.

ROBERT CARVER (1967–), CHANCELLOR KENT PROFESSOR
OF LAW AND LEGAL STUDIES AT YALE UNIVERSITY

———

Definitions are the foundation of reason. You can't reason without them.

ROBERT M. PIRSIG
Zen and the Art of Motorcycle Maintenance (1974)

It is likewise to be observed, that this society [the legal profession] hath a peculiar cant and jargon of their own, that no other mortal can understand, and wherein all their laws are written, which they take special care to multiply; whereby they have wholly confounded the very essence of truth and falsehood, of right and wrong; so that it will take thirty years to decide whether the field left me by my ancestors for six generations belongs to me, or to a stranger three hundred miles off.

JONATHAN SWIFT
Gulliver's Travels (1726)

There is something monstrous in commands couched in invented and unfamiliar language; an alien master is the worst of all. The language of the law must not be foreign to the ears of those who are to obey it.

LEARNED HAND, SPEECH IN WASHINGTON, D.C. (MAY 11, 1929)

Let all the laws be clear, uniform, and precise; to interpret laws is almost always to corrupt them.

VOLTAIRE
Philosophical Dictionary (1764)

From the very beginning, our state and national constitutions and laws have laid great emphasis on procedural and substantive safeguards designed to assure fair trials before impartial tribunals in which every defendant stands equal before the law. This noble ideal cannot be realized if the poor man charged with a crime has to face his accusers without a lawyer to assist him.

U.S. SUPREME COURT JUSTICE HUGO BLACK
Gideon v. Wainwright (1963)

Today there's law and order in everything. You can't beat anybody for nothing. If you do beat anyone, it's got to be for the sake of order.

MAXIM GORKY
The Lower Depths (1903)

———

Not everyone is playing by the Marquis of Queensberry rules.

PORTER J. GOSS (1938–), CHAIRMAN OF THE HOUSE INTELLIGENCE COMMITTEE, ON PROPOSALS TO EASE RESTRICTIONS ON C.I.A. ACTIVITIES IN ORDER TO COMBAT TERRORISM

It could only be the record of what had had to be done, and what assuredly would have to be done again in the never ending fight against terror and its relentless onslaughts, despite their personal afflictions, by all who while unable to be saints but refusing to bow down to pestilences, strive their utmost to be healers.

Albert Camus
The Plague (1957)

The law is the difference between a debate and an alley fight.

ROBERT TRAVER
The Jealous Mistress (1967)

Possession is nine tenths of the law.

LORD MANSFIELD (1728)

The more laws, the more offenders.

THOMAS FULLER, M. D.
Gnomologia (1732)

The customs, beliefs, or needs of a primitive time establish a rule or a formula. In the course of centuries the custom, belief, or necessity disappears, but the rule remains. The reason which gave rise to the rule has been forgotten, and ingenious minds set themselves to inquire how it is to be accounted for.

U.S. SUPREME COURT JUSTICE OLIVER WENDELL HOLMES, JR.
(1841–1935)

We have several set forms which are held as law, and so held and used for good reason, though we cannot at present remember that reason.

CHIEF JUSTICE FORTESCUE (1458)

It is a maxim among these lawyers, that whatever hath been done before, may legally be done again: and therefore they take special care to record all the decisions formerly made against common justice, and the general reason of mankind. These, under the name of precedents, they produce as authorities, to justify the most iniquitous opinions . . .

JONATHAN SWIFT
Gulliver's Travels (1726)

Nothing is more common, in the history of mankind, then a servile adoption of received opinions, and a timid acquiescence in whatever is established. It matters not, whether a doctrine or institution owes its existence to accident or design, to wisdom or ignorance, or folly, there is a natural tendency to give it undue value in proportion to its antiquity.

JOSEPH STORY (1779–1845), IN A SPEECH TO THE
PHI BETTA KAPPA SOCIETY OF HARVARD

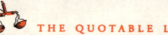

All bad precedents began as justifiable measures.

JULIUS CAESAR, QUOTED IN SALLUST'S *Conspiracy of Catiline*
(1ST CENTURY B.C.)

No doubt one may quote history to support any cause, as the devil quotes the scripture.

LEARNED HAND
Sources of Tolerance (1930)

Laws that only threaten, and are not kept, become like the log that was given to the frogs to be their king, which they feared at first, but soon scorned and trampled on.

CERVANTES
Don Quixote (1604)

I'm not an Uncle Tom ... I'm going to be here for forty years. For those who don't like it, get over it.

U.S. SUPREME COURT JUSTICE CLARENCE THOMAS (1948–)

Anyone who takes it upon himself, on his private authority, to break a bad law, thereby authorizes everyone else to break the good ones.

DENIS DIDEROT
SUPPLEMENT TO BOUGAINVILLE'S *Voyage* (1796)

It usually takes a hundred years to make a law, and then, after it has done its work, it usually takes a hundred years to get rid of it.

HENRY WARD BEECHER
Proverbs from Plymouth Pulpit (1847)

Nobody has a more sacred obligation to obey the law than those who make the law.

JEAN ANOUILH
Antigone (1939)

Green fumbled, and seemed to accidentally shut the Bible, whereupon visiting legal dignitaries grinned and nudged each other, for this was a venerable court-room ploy—the lawyer who while reading from the Scriptures pretends to lose his place, and then remarks, as Green now did, "Never mind. I think I can quote from memory. Genesis Nine, Verse Six: 'Whoso sheddeth man's blood, by man shall his blood be shed.'"

TRUMAN CAPOTE
In Cold Blood (1966)

A lawyer should assist the legal profession in fulfilling its duty to make legal counsel available.

THE NEW YORK STATE BAR ASSOCIATION, *CANON 2, The Lawyer's Code of Professional Responsibility* (1999)

For the conventionalities of the law he entertained a supreme contempt, but he did wish so to arrange matters with which he was himself concerned as to do what justice demanded.

ANTHONY TROLLOPE
Orley Farm (1854)

Men, I think, are ever attracted to the *bon mot* rather than the *mot juste*, and judges, no less than other men, are often moved by considerations more aesthetic than judicial.

JOHN BARTH (1930–)
The Floating Opera (N.D.)

We live in the midst of the common law; we inhale it at every breath, imbibe it at every pore; we meet with it when we wake and when we lie down to sleep, when we travel and when we stay at home; and it is inter-woven with the very idiom that we speak and we cannot learn another system of laws, without at the same time, another language.

CHANCELLOR JAMES KENT (1763–1847)

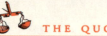

How each participant "performs" can be important, for a judgment can depend not only on what is said but also on the way it is expressed. The good lawyer is a skillful director as well as author, carefully rehearsing his or her presentation and witnesses, even deciding what clothing (perhaps *costume* is the better word) they should wear in court to enhance their case.

CARL SMITH
Law as Form and Theme in American Letters (1927)

Whenever he (or she) organizes his material into persuasive form and addresses the audience he wishes to move, the lawyer gives himself a character and establishes, for the moment at least, a relation with his audience, as well as with his client. What kind of character, what kind of community, does he—can he—establish in these ways? What sort of truth, or justice, or beauty, can he be said to serve?

JAMES BOYD WHITE (1939–)
Hercules's Bow (N.D.)

Green, a suavely tough little septuagenarian, has an imposing reputation among his peers, who admire his stagecraft—a repertoire of actorish gifts that includes a sense of timing as acute as a nightclub comedian's. An expert criminal lawyer, his usual role is that of defender, but in this instance the state had retained him as a special assistant to Duane West, for it felt that the young county attorney was too unseasoned to prosecute the case without experienced support.

TRUMAN CAPOTE
In Cold Blood (1966)

The defense is not actually permitted by the Law, but only tolerated.

FRANZ KAFKA
The Trial (1925)

Wooten's strategy was to pick one member [of the jury] who was strong and intelligent and one who, in his opinion, wasn't. You tried to present your case in story form to the juror who was not intelligent, whereas you argued the contradictions before the one who was.

NORMAN MAILER
The Executioner's Song (1990)

Jarndyce and Jarndyce drones on. This scarecrow of a suit has, in course of time, become so complicated, that no man alive knows what it means. The parties to it understand it least; but it has been observed that no two Chancery lawyers can talk about it for five minutes, without coming to a total disagreement as to all the premises. Innumerable children have been born into the cause; innumerable young people have married into it; innumerable old people have died out of it. Scores of persons have deliriously found themselves made particed in Jarndyce and Jarndyce, without knowing how or why; whole families have inherited legendary hatreds with the suit. The little plaintiff or defendant, who was promised a new rocking-horse when Jarndyce and Jarndyce would be settled, has grown up, possessed himself of a real horse, and trotted away into the other world.

CHARLES DICKENS
Bleak House (1853)

There are ever increasing ways in which witnesses can be wounded in the course of cross-examination. Within the rules, it is the trial lawyer's job to inflict that wound on the adverse witness.

ROBERT GOLDMAN
The Modern Art of Cross-Examination (1993)

And remember, Robert, when you have finshed your oral argument, don't trail off, or glance at your notes for some afterthought or final emphasis, but obey the immortal command of the late John W. Davis, the greatest pleader it was ever my privilege to hear— here the ready voice becomes suddenly stentorian— "and sit down!"

LOUIS AUCHINCLOSS
Diary of a Yuppie (1986)

We ask him [the accused] whether or not he confesses his guilt in a foolish way, tending to induce him to deny it; but that is not much. Guilt seldom will confess as long as a chance remains. But we teach him to lie, or rather we lie for him during the whole ceremony of his trial. We think it merciful to five him chances of escape, and hunt him as we do a fox, in obedience to certain laws framed for his protection.

ANTHONY TROLLOPE
Orley Farm (1854)

Poor bastard's got himself up for a real performance and the place, the whole atmosphere's like a theatre but they're not there for a matinee and this whole star turn goes out the window, a few more questions and down comes the curtain.

TOM WOLFE
Bonfire of the Vanities (1987)

That remark of the Judge's has no significance for you ... Don't get into a panic at every word. If you do it again I'll never tell you anything ... All that I said was to report a remark by a Judge. You know quite well that in these matters opinions differ so much that the confusion is impenetrable. This judge, for instance, assumes that the proceedings begin at one point, and I assume that they begin at another point. A difference of opinion, nothing more.

FRANZ KAFKA
The Trial (1925)

The judge is always a person deciding a case the story of which can be characterized in a rich range of ways; and he (or she) is always responsible both for his choice of characterization and for his decision. He is always responsible as a composer for the composition he makes.

JAMES BOYD WHITE (1939–)
The Judicial Opinion and the Poem (N.D.)

Everything belongs to the court.

FRANZ KAFKA
The Trial (1925)

In the heels of the haggling lawyers, Bob,
Too many slippery ifs and buts and howevers,
Too much hereinbefore provided whereas,
Too many doors to go in and out of.

CARL SANDBURG (1878-1967)

It is at the moment when experience turns to instinct that a good trial lawyer or cross-examiner is developed.

ROBERT GOLDMAN
The Modern Art of Cross-Examination (1993)

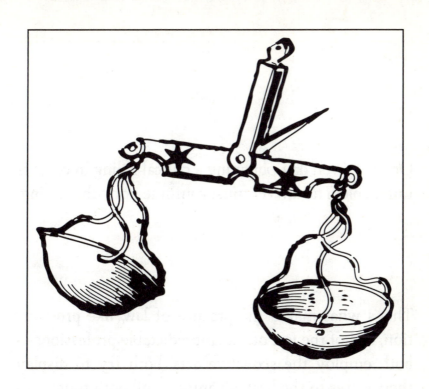

4

The Practice of Law

On any given day, obtaining a critical ruling in court is unreliable. The lawyer must continue notwithstanding.

ROBERT GOLDMAN
The Modern Art of Cross-Examination (1993)

That's what makes the practice of law, like prostitution, one of the last of the unpredictable professions—both employ the seductive arts, both try to display their wares to the best advantage, and both must pretend enthusiastically to woo total strangers.

ROBERT TRAVER
Anatomy of a Murder (1958)

The law offers greater opportunities to be at one and the same time a Christian and a horse-trader than any other profession.

ARTHUR TRAIN
The Adventures of Ephraim Tutt (1939)

I will not say ... that "The law will admit of no rival," but I will say that it is a jealous mistress, and requires a long and constant courtship. It is not to be won by trifling favors ...

JOSEPH STORY (1779–1845)

The law is a jealous mistress.

AUTHOR PROBABLY UNKNOWN, THE PHRASE BEING VARIOUSLY ATTRIB-
UTED TO NUMEROUS OLD-TIME LAWYERS, JUDGES, AND LEGAL SCHOL-
ARS, INCLUDING THE ENGLISHMAN ROGER NORTH IN 1824 AND THE
AMERICAN JOSEPH STORY IN 1829.

The lawyer's truth is not Truth, but consistency, or a
consistent expediency. Truth is always in harmony
with herself, and is not concerned chiefly to reveal the
justice that may consist with wrongdoing.

HENRY DAVID THOREAU (1817–1862)

Every legal case that ever happened is essentially a story, the story of aroused, pulsing, actual people fighting each other or the state for *something*: for money, for property, for power, pride, honor, love, freedom, even for life—and quite often, one suspects, for the pure unholy joy of fighting.

ROBERT TRAVER
The Jealous Mistress (1967)

We lawyers are always curious, always inquisitive, always picking up odds and ends for our patchwork minds, since there is no knowing when and where they may fit into some corner.

CHARLES DICKENS
Little Dorritt (1857)

There are more lawyers just in Washington, D.C. than in all of Japan. They've got about as many lawyers as we have sumo wrestlers.

LEE IACOCCA (1924–)
ON THE LACK OF LITIGATION AMONG JAPANESE BUSINESSES

The trial lawyer does what Socrates was executed for: making the worse argument appear the stronger.

JUDGE IRVING KAUFMAN (1910–1992)

A lawyer should assist in maintaining the integrity and competence of the legal profession.

THE NEW YORK STATE BAR ASSOCIATION
The Lawyer's Code of Professional Responsibility (1999)

I don't want a lawyer to tell me what I cannot do; I hire him to tell me how to do what I want to do.

J. PIERPONT MORGAN (1837–1913)

Mr. Jaggers was altogether too many for the jury, and they gave in.

WEMMICK, OF LAWYER JAGGERS,
CHARLES DICKENS, *Great Expectations* (1861)

If in your own judgment you cannot be an honest lawyer, resolve to be honest without being a lawyer.

PRESIDENT ABRAHAM LINCOLN (1809–1865)

[A lawyer's] performance in the courtroom is responsible for about 25 percent of the outcome; the remaining 75 percent depends upon the facts.

MELVIN BELLI
US News & World Report (September 20, 1982)

A lawyer's not a person who knows the law; a lawyer is a person who's learned how to find the law that's needed in a given situation. And also how to read it, a correlative that some lawyers overlook, to the sorrow of their clients.

GEORGE V. HIGGINS
Sandra Nichols Found Dead (1996)

There are two qualities that make for the highest success in the law—honesty and dishonesty. To get ahead you must either be so irreproachable in your conduct and elevated in your ideals that your reputation for viture becomes your chief asset, or, on the other hand, so crooked that your very dishonesty makes you invaluable to your clients . . . the crooked lawyer has got to be so crooked that everybody is afraid of him, even the judge.

ARTHUR TRAIN
The Confessions of Artemas Quibble (1911)

Ours is a sick profession marked by incompetence, lack of training, misconduct and bad manners. Ineptness, bungling, malpractice, and bad ethics can be observed in court houses all over this country every day... these incompetents have a seeming unawareness of the fundamental ethics of the profession.

U.S. CHIEF JUSTICE WARREN E. BURGER (1907–1995)

Imagine the appeals, dissents, and remandments,
If lawyers had written the Ten Commandments.

GEORGE HARRISON "HARRY" BENDER (1896–1961)

Never stir up litigation. A worse man can scarcely be
found than one who does this. Who can be more near-
ly a fiend than he who habitually overhauls the regis-
ter of deeds in search of defects in titles, whereon to
stir up strife, and put money in his pocket?

PRESIDENT ABRAHAM LINCOLN (1809–1865)

A lawyer is never entirely comfortable with a friendly divorce, any more than a good mortician wants to finish his job and then have the patient sit up on the table.

JEAN KERR (1923–)

Lawyers are just like physicians: what one says, the other contradicts.

SHOLOM ALEICHEM (*pseudonym of* SOLOMON J. RABINOWITZ) (1859–1916)

A lawyer is one whose opinion is worth nothing unless paid for.

ENGLISH PROVERB

———

The leading rule for the lawyer, as for the man of every other calling, is diligence. Leave nothing for to-morrow which can be done to-day.

PRESIDENT ABRAHAM LINCOLN (1809–1865)

He is no lawyer who cannot take two sides.

CHARLES LAMB (1775–1834)

A criminal lawyer, like a trapeze performer, is seldom more than one slip from an awful fall.

PAUL O'NEIL (1952–)

I am a trial lawyer. Matilda says that at dinner on a good day I sound like an affidavit.

MARIO CUOMO (1932–)
FORMER GOVERNOR OF NEW YORK STATE

But in the last analysis it is the desire for the respect and confidence of the members of the profession and of the society which the lawyer serves that should provide to a lawyer the incentive for the highest possible degree of ethical conduct. The possible loss of that respect and confidence is the ultimate sanction. So long as its practitioners are guided by these principles, the law will continue to be a noble profession.

THE NEW YORK STATE BAR ASSOCIATION
The Lawyer's Code of Professional Responsibility (1999)

No splints yet invented will heal a lawyer's broken reputation.

PAUL O'NEIL (1952–)

———

Law students are trained in the case method, and to the lawyer everything in life looks like a case.

EDWARD PACKARD, JR.
Columbia Forum (1967)

If there is any truth to the old proverb that "One who is his own lawyer has a fool for a client," the Court now bestows a constitutional right on one to make a fool of himself.

U.S. SUPREME COURT JUSTICE HARRY A. BLACKMUN (1908–1999)

What a holler would ensue if people had to pay the minister as much to marry them as they have to pay a lawyer to get them a divorce.

CLAIRE TREVOR (1909–2000)

The upbeat lawyer/negotiator of preadolescence has become a real pro by now—cynical, shrewd, a tough cookie. You're constantly embroiled in a match of wits. You're exhausted.

RON TAFFEL, PH.D. (1942–)

Although the lawyer has the duty to represent the client zealously, the lawyer should not engage in any conduct that offends the dignity and decorum of proceedings.

THE NEW YORK STATE BAR ASSOCIATION
The Lawyer's Code of Professional Responsibility (1999)

The good lawyer is the great salesman.

U.S. ATTORNEY GENERAL JANET RENO (1938–)

The good lawyer is not the man who has an eye to every side and angle of contingency, and qualifies all his qualifications, but who throws himself on your part so heartily, that he can get you out of a scrape.

RALPH WALDO EMERSON (1803–1882)

Resolve to be honest at all events; and if in your own judgment you cannot be an honest lawyer, resolve to be honest without being a lawyer. Choose some other occupation, rather than one in the choosing of which you do, in advance, consent to be a knave.

PRESIDENT ABRAHAM LINCOLN (1809–1865)

Why may not that be the skull of a lawyer? Where be his quiddities now, his quillets, his cases, his tenures, and his tricks?

WILLIAM SHAKESPEARE
Hamlet. Act v. Sc. 1 (c. 1601)

He wanted law from a lawyer as he wanted a coat from a tailor, because he could not make it so well himself.

ANTHONY TROLLOPE
The Warden (1855)

———

Don't fear the law, fear lawyers.

OLD RUSSIAN PROVERB

When you go into an attorney's office door, you will have to pay for it, first or last.

ANTHONY TROLLOPE (1815–1882)

Extemporaneous speaking should be practiced and cultivated. It is the lawyer's avenue to the public . . . And yet there is not a more fatal error to young lawyers than relying too much on speechmaking. If any one, upon his rare powers of speaking, shall claim an exemption from the drudgery of the law, his case is a failure in advance.

PRESIDENT ABRAHAM LINCOLN (1809–1865)

A lawyer should preserve the confidences and secrets of a client.

THE NEW YORK STATE BAR ASSOCIATION, Canon 4, *The Lawyer's Code of Professional Responsibility* (1999)

A thought that cannot be expressed is no thought at all.

PHILIP H. PHENIX
Man and His Becoming (1964)

Always be spontaneous, but study hard so that your spontaneous opinions are wise.

SAMUEL TAYLOR COLERIDGE (1772–1834)

It is better to be lucky. But I would rather be exact. Then when luck comes you are ready.

ERNEST HEMINGWAY
The Old Man and the Sea (1952)

He wanted the rapes, the murders, the child abuses, the ugly causes no one else wanted. He waned to be a civil rights lawyer and litigate civil liberties. But most of all Lucien wanted to be a radical, a flaming radical of a lawyer with unpopular cases and causes, and lots of attention.

JOHN GRISHAM
A Time to Kill (1987)

Nothing, not even an unending string of personal tragedies, deterred him from giving each client a full measure of dedication or caused him to cross the line to questionable practice.

ROBERT GOLDMAN
The Modern Art of Cross-Examination (1993)

A lawyer shall not give or lend anything of value to a judge, official, or employee of a tribunal . . .

THE NEW YORK STATE BAR ASSOCIATION
The Lawyer's Code of Professional Responsibility (1999)

A lawyer's either a social engineer or he's a parasite on society.

CHARLES HOUSTON (1895–1950)
FORMER DEAN OF HOWARD UNIVERSITY

No one is under pressure. There wasn't a light on when I left at 2 o'clock this morning.

HOYT A. MOORE, QUOTED BY A PARTNER IN HIS MANHATTAN LAW FIRM CRAVATH, SWAINE & MOORE, *Time* (June 24, 1964)

Before the Law stands a gatekeeper. To this doorkeeper there comes a man from the country who begs for admittance to the Law. But the doorkeeper says that he cannot admit the man at the moment. The man, on reflection, asks if he will be allowed, then, to enter later. "It is possible," answers the doorkeeper, "but not at this moment."

FRANZ KAFKA
The Trial (1925)

I am a man who, from his youth upwards, has been filled with the profound conviction that the easiest way in life is the best. Hence, though I belong to a profession proverbially energetic and nervous, even to turbulence, at times, yet nothing of that sort have I ever suffered to invade my peace. I am one of those unambitious lawyers who never addresses a jury, or in any way draws down public applause; but, in the cool tranquility of a snug retreat, do a snug business among rich men's bonds, and mortgages, and title-deeds. All who know me, consider me an eminently safe man.

HERMAN MELVILLE
Bartleby, The Scrivener (1859)

Upchurch was a lawyer who wanted to be seen and heard in magazine articles, news stories, advice columns, quickie books, and gossip shows . . . He grinned at himself in the mirror as he tied his ninety-dollar tie and thought of spending the next six months in New Orleans with the press at his beck and call. This was why he went to law school!

JOHN GRISHAM
The Client (1993)

When an action in the best interest of the client seems to the lawyer to be unjust, the lawyer may ask the client for permission to forgo such action.

THE NEW YORK STATE BAR ASSOCIATION
The Lawyer's Code of Professional Responsibility (1999)

The traditional process of making students "think like a lawyer" has disconnected them from real world thinking, which is one of the reasons the students hate law school in the first place. Sensing that something is terribly wrong, law students see law and literature as a way of relearning modes of thought that have practical value to them.

JOHN JAY OSBORN (1929–1994)

No one can be a truly competent lawyer unless he is a cultivated man. The best way to come to the study of law is to come to the study of law as a well-read person.

U.S. SUPREME COURT JUSTICE FELIX FRANKFURTER (1882–1965)
LETTER TO STUDENT

Both strands of learning, the literary and the legal, concern themselves with the dilemma of the human condition. The consequences of individual decisions and actions, the tolerance of conflicting views, the balancing of justice and mercy, freedom and authority. These themes are the grist of the novelist's imagination, the poet's vision, the essayist's insight, no less than a lawyer's craft.

JAMES O. FREEDMAN (1936–)
ATTORNEY AND PRESIDENT OF DARTMOUTH COLLEGE

Write an opinion, and read it a few years later when it is dissected in the briefs of counsel. You will learn for the first time the limitations of the powers of speech . . . All sorts of gaps and obstacles . . . will obtrude themselves before your gaze . . . Sometimes you will feel the fault is with counsel who have stupidly misread the obvious, in which event . . . you will be solaced, even in your chagrin, but a sense of injured innocence. Sometimes . . . you will even believe that the misreading is less stupid than malicious, in which event you will be wise to keep your feelings to yourself.

BENJAMIN CARDOZO
Law and Literature and Other Essays (1931)

The system today does not permit the long nurturing process that so often formed trial lawyers in past years . . . They were forced to endure a salary which never came close to meeting their expenses in recognition of the fact that the experience that they were being given and the responsibilities with which they were being entrusted were worth more than dollars at the present moment.

ROBERT GOLDMAN
The Modern Art of Cross-Examination (1993)

Your lawyer in practice spends a considerable part of his life doing distasteful things for disagreeable people who must be satisfied against an impossible time limit and with hourly interruptions from other disagreeable people who want to derail the train; and for his blood, sweat, and tears he receives in the end a few unkind words to the effect that it might have been done better, and a protest at the size of the fee.

WILLIAM L. PROSSER (1898–)

5

Law, Money, and Power

The poor man looks upon the law as an enemy, not as a friend. For him the law is always taking something away.

ATTORNEY GENERAL ROBERT F. KENNEDY
LAW DAY SPEECH (MAY 1, 1964)

It is a measure of the framers' fear that a passing majority might find it expedient to compromise 4th Amendment values that these values were embodied in the Constitution itself.

U.S. SUPREME COURT JUSTICE SANDRA DAY O'CONNOR, DISSENTING OPINION IN 5-4 RULING THAT BROADENED AN EXCEPTION TO THE 4TH AMENDMENT RULE BARRING USE OF UNCONSTITUTIONALLY SEIZED EVIDENCE IN CRIMINAL TRIALS (1987)

There can be no equal justice where the kind of trial a man gets depends on the amount of money he has.

U.S. SUPREME COURT JUSTICE HUGO BLACK
Griffin v. Illinois (1964)

In respect of civil rights, all citizens are equal before the law. The humblest is the peer of the most powerful.

U.S. SUPREME COURT JUSTICE JOHN HARLAN
Plessey v. Ferguson [DISSENT] (1896)

Nine tenths of you are in jail because you did not have a good lawyer and, of course, you did not have a good lawyer because you did not have enough money to pay a good lawyer.

CLARENCE DARROW
*Address to the Prisoners in the Cook County Jail (*1902)

The legal profession owes it to itself that wrongs do not go without a remedy because the injured has no advocate . . . Does the lawyer ask, Who is my neighbor? I answer—the poor man deprived of his just dues.

CHARLES EVANS HUGHES
SPEECH TO THE AMERICAN BAR ASSOCIATION (AUGUST 1920)

To such a height th' Expence of courts is gone, That poor Men are redress'd — till they're undone.

BENJAMIN FRANKLIN
Poor Richard's Almanack (1733)

Except for the few that legal services lawyers can represent, poor people have access to American courts in the same sense that the Christians had access to the lions when they were dragged, unarmed, into a Roman arena.

EARL JOHNSON, JR. (1934–)

People say law, but they mean wealth.

RALPH WALDO EMERSON (1803–1882)

And what is truth?
Is truth unchanging laws?
We both have truths;
Are mine the same as yours?

PONTIUS PILATE, SPEAKING TO JESUS AT HIS TRIAL
FROM *Jesus Christ Superstar* BY ANDREW LLOYD WEBBER
AND TIM RICE (1970)

Laws grind the poor, and rich men rule the law.

OLIVER GOLDSMITH (1728–1774)

Laws are necessary to protect the feeble against the violence of the strong.

JAMES FENIMORE COOPER (1789–1851)

Riches without law are more dangerous than is poverty without law.

HENRY WARD BEECHER (1813–1887)

The poor are not oppressed, the rich are not privileged . . . there is nothing [in America] to engender riots and tumults.

THOMAS PAINE
The Rights of Man (1792)

Justice is open to everyone in the same way as the Ritz Hotel.

JUDGE STURGESS (JULY 22, 1928)

A man's respect for law and order exists in precise relationship to the size of his paycheck.

ADAM CLAYTON POWELL, JR. (1908–1972)

There is more power in socially organized masses on the march than there is in guns in the hands of a few desperate men.

MARTIN LUTHER KING, JR. (1929–1968)

What distinguished Reagan's America was that the very rich became much richer, while the difference between those who prospered and those who didn't . . . became demonstrably wider.

LOU CANNON (1938–)

Jerome Clifford had been defending prominent New Orleans thugs for fifteen years—gangsters, pushers, politicians—and his record was impressive. He was cunning and corrupt, completely willing to buy people who could be bought. He drank with judges and slept with their girlfriends. He bribed the cops and threatened the jurors.

John Grisham
The Client (1993)

My hope is that ten years from now, after I've been across the street at work for a while, they'll all be glad they gave me that wonderful vote.

U.S. SUPREME COURT JUSTICE SANDRA DAY O'CONNOR, ON BEING CONFIRMED UNANIMOUSLY BY THE SENATE (SEPTEMBER 21, 1981)

There are mighty historical and economic forces that keep the poor down; and there are human beings who help out in this grim business, many of them unwittingly.

MICHAEL HARRINGTON
The Other America: Poverty in the United States (1962)

The Golden Rule says that he who has the gold makes the rules.

ANONYMOUS

At least seven members of Congress receive thousands of dollars in farm subsidies each year, and all but two sit on the agriculture committees that are writing the new farm policy.

The New York Times

Across the world . . . the correlation between political freedom and prosperity is a close one.

The Economist (1994)

Generally and perhaps not accidentally, the attributes of the poor—inadequate education, old age, poor health, and so forth—have been incorrectly viewed as the causes of poverty.

PAMELA ROBY

QUOTED IN EDWARD WEISBAND'S *Poverty Amidst Plenty* (1989)

Misery generates social chaos, and it takes money just to police it, just to keep it from becoming so explosive that it will disturb the tranquility of the better off. In cold cash-and-carry terms, there would be a long-range pay-off if slums were abolished . . .

MICHAEL HARRINGTON
The Other America: Poverty in the United States (1962)

A rising star among the gang of boisterous mouth-pieces trotting across the country performing for crooks and cameras . . . He had become somewhat rich and noted in Chicago for his passionate defense of mob assassins and drug traffickers.

JOHN GRISHAM
The Client (1993)

———

The power to tax is not the power to destroy while this Court sits.

U.S. SUPREME COURT JUSTICE OLIVER WENDELL HOLMES, JR.
(1841–1935)

Offenders of upper status backgrounds are given less severe sanctions than members of minority groups and lower class.

GEORGE F. COLE
The American System of Criminal Justice (2000)

It's easy to see how to do away with what we call crime. It is not so easy to do it. I will tell you how to do it. It can be done by giving people a chance to live—by destroying special privileges. So long as big criminals can get the coal fields, so long as the big criminals have control of the city council and get the public streets for streetcars and gas rights—this is bound to send thousands of poor people to jail. So long as men are allowed to monopolize the earth, and compel others to live on such terms as these men see fit to make, then you are bound to get into jail.

CLARENCE DARROW
Address to the Prisoners in the Cook County Jail (1902)

It just takes one, he says over and over. You hear all the time in this business. One big case, and you can retire. That's the reason lawyers do so many sleazy things, like full-color ads in the Yellow Pages, and billboards, and placards on city buses, and telephone solicitation. You hold your nose, ignore the stench of what you're doing, ignore the snubs and snobbery of big-firm lawyers, because it only takes one.

JOHN GRISHAM
The Rainmaker (1995)

Were there arguments in his favor that had been over-looked? Of course there must be. Logic is unshakeable, but it cannot withstand a man who wantes to go on living. Where was the Judge whom he had never seen? Where was the High Court, to which he had never penetrated?

FRANZ KAFKA
The Trial (1925)

Two bars of solid gold shone on the ground before them, a prize for the judge who'd speak the straightest verdict.

HOMER (C. 850 B.C.– ?)
The Iliad

Was Hamlet guilty or not by reason of insanity for the murder of Polonius? The millionaire tells me how happy he is to meet me. He wishes me luck. He wants to know what I think of Hamlet's case. He tells me Hamlet is responsible for what he did, insane or not.

SHERMAN ALEXIE
At the Trial of Hamlet (1994)

6

Justice and Injustice

Justice is indiscriminately due to all, without regard to numbers, wealth, or rank.

JOHN JAY (1745–1829)

In my time I have seen truth that was anything under the sun but just, and I have seen justice using tools and instruments I wouldn't want to touch with a ten-foot fence rail.

WILLIAM FAULKNER
Knight's Gambit (1949)

I expect to see the day when women serve the cause of Justice in numbers fully reflective of their talent. That day, when bias, conscious or unconscious, is no longer part of the scene, has already dawned in some places.

U.S. SUPREME COURT JUSTICE RUTH BADER GINSBURG,
SPEECH GIVEN AT WELLESLEY COLLEGE (NOVEMBER 13, 1998)

The lawyer is the fellow who evens things up, the champion of all those who . . . must bear the whips and scorns of time, the oppressor's wrong. . .the law's delay. . . . He fights fire with fire, meets guile with guile, and rights the legal wrong.

ARTHUR TRAIN
Mr. Tutt's Case Book (1936)

Statutes authorizing unreasonable searches were the core concern of the framers of the 4th Amendment.

U.S. SUPREME COURT JUSTICE SANDRA DAY O'CONNOR (1987)

The first duty of society is justice.

ALEXANDER HAMILTON (1757–1804)

Justice, sir, is the great interest of man on this earth. It is the ligament which holds civilized beings and civilized nations together.

DANIEL WEBSTER (SEPTEMBER 12, 1845)

Justice, and only justice, shall always be our motto.

PRESIDENT WOODROW WILSON
INAUGURAL ADDRESS (MARCH 14, 1913)

If the motto "and justice for all" becomes "and justice for those who can afford it," we threaten the very underpinnings of our social contract.

RONALD GEORGE, CHIEF JUSTICE OF THE CALIFORNIA SUPREME
COURT, ANNUAL STATE OF THE JUDICIARY SPEECH (2001)

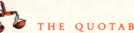

If particular care and attention is not paid to the ladies, we are determined to foment a rebellion, and will not hold ourselves bound by any laws in which we have no voice or representation.

ABIGAIL ADAMS (1744–1818)

A man who graduated high in his class at Yale Law School and made partnership in a top law firm would be celebrated. A man who invested wisely would be admired, but a woman who accomplishes this is treated with suspicion.

BARBRA STREISAND, SINGER AND ACTRESS, ON HILLARY RODHAM CLINTON, QUOTED IN *The New York Times* (APRIL 16, 1994).

Equality before the law in a true democracy is a matter of right. It cannot be a matter of charity or of favor or of grace or of discretion.

U.S. SUPREME COURT JUSTICE WILEY RUTLEDGE
SPEECH TO THE AMERICAN BAR ASSOCIATION (SEPTEMBER 29, 1941)

Lawyers are operators of toll bridges across which anyone in search of justice must pass.

JANE BRYANT QUINN
Newsweek (October 9, 1978)

Concepts of justice must have hands and feet to carry out justice in every case in the shortest possible time and at the lowest possible cost. This is the challenge to every lawyer and judge in America.

U.S. CHIEF JUSTICE WARREN E. BURGER (1907–1995)

Truth and justice are ultimate values, so understood by our people, and the law and the legal profession will not be worthy of public respect and loyalty if we allow our attention to be diverted from these goals.

DALLIN H. OAKS (1932–)

"If the law supposes that," said Mr. Bumble, "the law is an ass."

CHARLES DICKENS (1812–1870)

Oh judgment thou are fled to brutish beasts, and men have lost their reason.

WILLIAM SHAKESPEARE (1564–1616)

I want him. I want justice. And there's an old poster out West, as I recall, that said: Wanted: Dead or Alive.

PRESIDENT GEORGE W. BUSH (1946–)

Each lawyer's own conscience must provide the touch-stone against which to test the extent to which the lawyer's actions should rise above minimum standards.

THE NEW YORK STATE BAR ASSOCIATION
The Lawyer's Code of Professional Responsibility (1999)

Much of what history relates . . . chills, shames, and disgusts us.

RUFUS CHOATE (1799–1859)

Laws are to govern all alike—those opposed as well as those who favor them. I know of no method to repeal bad or obnoxious laws so effective as their stringent execution.

PRESIDENT ULYSSES S. GRANT
FIRST INAUGURAL ADDRESS (MARCH 4, 1869)

An unjust law is no law at all.

ST. AUGUSTINE (? –604)

Only the wise are just.

HENRY DAVID THOREAU (1817–1862)

A lawyer has no business with the justice or injustice of the cause which he undertakes, unless his client asks his opinion, and then he is bound to give it honestly. The justice or injustice of the cause is to be decided by the judge.

JAMES BOSWELL
Journal of a Tour to the Hebrides (1785)

Justice without might is helpless; might without justice is tyrannical.

BLAISE PASCAL (1623–1662)

I submit that an individual who breaks a law that con-science tells him is unjust, and who willingly accepts the penalty of imprisonment in order to arouse the conscience of the community over its injustice, is in reality expressing the highest respect for the law.

MARTIN LUTHER KING, JR. (1929–1968)

In a world that is largely unfair, you make your choices.

GEORGE YONEMURA'S FATHER

And he who goes the furthest, and does the worst, only uses within limits the power that the law gives him.

HARRIET BEECHER STOWE
Uncle Tom's Cabin (1852)

I don't want to live in accordance with circumstances, conventions and material expediency, but I want to live and struggle for what seems to me to be just and right without regard to consequences.

IGNAZIO SILONE
Bread and Wine (1937)

Injustice anywhere is a threat to justice everywhere.

MARTIN LUTHER KING, JR. (1929–1968)

Our Constitution is color-blind, and neither knows nor tolerates classes among citizens.

U.S. SUPREME COURT JUSTICE JOHN MARSHALL HARLAN
Plessey v. Ferguson [DISSENT] (1896)

There is not under our Constitution a judicial remedy for every political mischief, for every undesirable exercise of legislative power.

U.S. SUPREME COURT JUSTICE FELIX FRANKFURTER
DISSENTING OPINION IN *Baker v. Carr* (1962)

Every man is equally entitled to protection by law.

PRESIDENT ANDREW JACKSON (1767–1845)

Separate educational facilities are inherently unequal.

U.S. CHIEF JUSTICE EARL WARREN
Brown v. Board of Education (1954)

The highest court in the land, the guardian of our national conscience, has reaffirmed its faith and the underlying American faith in the equality of all men and all children before the law.

The New York Times, COMMENTING ON THE DECISION IN
Brown v. Board of Education (MAY 18, 1954)

The fate of empires depends on the education of youth.

ARISTOTLE (384–322 B.C.)

Law and order are not here to be preserved by depriving the Negro children of their constitutional rights.

U.S. CHIEF JUSTICE EARL WARREN
Cooper v. Aaron (1958)

Non-violence is the first article of my creed. But I had either to submit to a system which I considered has done an irreparable harm to my country, or incur the risk of the mad fury of my people bursting forth when they understood the truth. I do not ask for mercy . . . I am here to invite and cheerfully submit to the highest penalty that can be inflicted for what in law is a deliberate crime and what appears to me to be the highest duty.

MOHANDAS K. GANDHI, AT HIS TRIAL FOR SEDITION IN 1922. HE WAS FOUND GUILTY AND SENTENCED TO SIX YEARS IN PRISON.

It might take plenty of sacrifice, but I don't think we'll ever again take such humiliating treatment as dished out by bus drivers in this city.

ROSA PARKS, MONTGOMERY, ALABAMA (1955)

That country is not mine which supports slavery.

HENRY DAVID THOREAU (1817–1862)

To live anywhere in the world today and be against equality because of race or color is like living in Alaska and being against snow.

WILLIAM FAULKNER
Essays (1965)

Congress, acting with its discretion and judgment, has the power under the Commerce Clause to ban racial discrimination.

U.S. SUPREME COURT JUSTICE HUGO BLACK
Heart of Atlanta Motel v. United States (1964)

During my lifetime I have dedicated myself to this struggle of the African people. I have fought against white domination and I have fought against black domination. I have cherished the ideal of a democratic and free society in which all persons live together in harmony and with equal opportunities. It is an ideal which I hope to live for and achieve. But, if need be, it is an ideal for which I have prepared to die.

NELSON MANDELA AT HIS TRIAL IN 1963, AFTER WHICH HE WAS FOUND GUILTY AND SENTENCED TO LIFE IN PRISON

Where segregation exists we must be willing to rise up . . . I realize that this type of courage means suffering and sacrifice. It might mean going to jail. If such is the case we must honorably fill up the jails of the South.

MARTIN LUTHER KING, JR. (1929–1968)

Under a government which imprisons any unjustly, the true place for a just man is also in prison.

HENRY DAVID THOREAU (1817–1862)

White and colored Piedmont got along pretty well in those years . . . as long as colored people didn't try to sit down in the Cut-Rate or at the Rendezvous Bar, or eat pizza at Eddie's, or buy property, or move into white neighborhoods, or dance with, date or dilate upon white people.

HENRY LOUIS GATES, JR.
Colored People (1995)

There can be do doubt that restricting the right to marry solely because of racial classifications violates the central meaning of the Equal Protection Clause.

U.S. CHIEF JUSTICE EARL WARREN
Loving v. Virginia (1967)

The world is shocked, or amused, by the sight of saintly old people hindering in the name of morality the removal of obvious brutalities from a legal system.

ALFRED NORTH WHITEHEAD
Adventure in Ideas (1933)

It is because of a legacy of unequal treatment that we now must permit the institutions of this society to give consideration to race in making decisions about who will hold the positions of influence, affluence, and prestige in America.

U.S. Supreme Court Justice Thurgood Marshall
Regents of the University of California v. Bakke (1978)

For the plague-stricken their peace of mind is more important than a human life. Decent folks must be allowed to sleep easy o'nights, mustn't they?

ALBERT CAMUS
The Plague (1957)

All Americans should be indignant when one American is denied the right to vote.

PRESIDENT LYNDON JOHNSON (1908–1973)

So long as the law considers all these human beings, with beating hearts and living affections, only as so many things belonging to a master—so long as the failure, or misfortune, or imprudence, or death of the kindest owner, may cause them any day to exchange a life of kind protection and indulgence for one of hopeless misery and toil—so long it is impossible to make anything beautiful or desirable in the best-regulated administration of slavery.

HARRIET BEECHER STOWE
Uncle Tom's Cabin (1852)

Each time a man stands up for an ideal, or acts to improve the lot of others, or strikes out against injustice, he sends a tiny ripple of hope, and crossing each other from a million different centers of energy and daring, these ripples will build a current which can sweep down the mightiest walls of oppression and resistance.

ATTORNEY GENERAL ROBERT F. KENNEDY (1925–1968)
SPEAKING IN SOUTH AFRICA

National injustice is the surest road to national downfall.

WILLIAM GLADSTONE (1809–1898)

There are not enough jails, not enough policemen, not enough courts to enforce a law not supported by the people.

HUBERT HUMPHREY
SPEECH AT WILLIAMSBURG, VIRGINIA (MAY 1, 1965)

The apprehended danger from the experiment of universal suffrage applied to the whole legislative department, is no dream of the imagination. It is too mighty an excitement for the moral condition of men to endure. The tendency of universal suffrage is to jeopardize the rights of property, and the principles of liberty. There is a constant tendency in human society, and the history of every age proves it; there is a constant tendency in the poor to covet and to share the plunder of the rich; in the debtor to relax or avoid the obligations of contract; the majority to tyrannize over the minority, and trample down their rights; in the indolent and profligate to caste the whole burthen of society upon the industrious and virtuous; and there is the tendency in ambitious and wicked men to inflame those combustible materials.

CHANCELLOR JAMES KENT (1763–1847)

Legislators represent people, not trees or acres. A citizen, a qualified voter, is no more nor less so because he lives in the city or on the farm.

U.S. CHIEF JUSTICE EARL WARREN
Reynolds v. Sims (1964)

There is no such thing as justice—in or out of court.

CLARENCE DARROW (1857–1938)

And thus I came to understand that I, anyhow, had had plague through all those long years in which, paradoxically enough, I'd believed with all my soul that I was fighting it. I learned that I had had an indirect hand in the deaths of thousands of people; that I'd even brought about their deaths by approving of acts and principles that could only end that way.

ALBERT CAMUS
The Plague (1957)

Justice is truth in action.

BENJAMIN DISRAELI (1804–1881)

Besides, all the people who are as alone as I am will one day gather at the river. We will watch the evening sun go down. And in the darkness maybe we will know the truth.

ALICE WALKER (1944–)

It is not desirable to cultivate a respect for the law so much as for the right.

HENRY DAVID THOREAU (1817–1862)

An unjust law is itself a species of violence. Arrest for its breach is more so.

MOHANDAS K. GANDHI
Non-Violence in Peace and War (1948)

Judicial decrees may not change the heart, but they can the restrain the heartless.

MARTIN LUTHER KING, JR. (1929–1968)

Slavery, as defined in American law, is no more capable of being regulated in its administration by principles of humanity, than the torture system of the Inquisition.

HARRIET BEECHER STOWE
A Key to Uncle Tom's Cabin (1852)

———

When we say "One Nation Under God, with liberty and justice for all," we are talking about all people. We either ought to believe it or quit saying it.

HUBERT HUMPHREY (1911–1978)

There are more issues and more problems and more needs, and once you are willing to take what is clearly the step that honesty and integrity require and become involved in these issues, there's never going to be any end to the demands.

NOAM CHOMSKY (1928–) ANSWERING BILL MOYERS'S QUESTION: WHAT PROPELLED YOU INTO ACTIVISM?

There seems no reason in principle why it should always be wrong to start a war. If other governments had foreseen what the Nazis would do, they would probably have been right to invade Germany to remove Hitler in the early 1930s.

JONATHAN GLOVER
Causing Death and Saving Lives (1977)

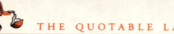
The dictum that truth always triumphs over persecution is one of those pleasant falsehoods which men repeat after one another till they pass into commonplaces, but which all experience refutes.

JOHN STUART MILL
On Liberty (1859)

If, at this critical moment, an able and ambitious man once gets power, he finds the way open for usurpations of every sort. So long as he sees to it for a certain time that material interests flourish, he can easily get away with everything else.

Alexis de Tocqueville
Democracy in America (1835)

Under the English legal system you are innocent until you are shown to be Irish.

TED WHITEHEAD (1900-1967)

Since when do you have to agree with people to defend them from injustice?

LILLIAN HELLMAN (1905–1984)

All lawful modes of expressing opposition to this principle had been closed by legislation, and we were placed in a position in which we had either to accept a permanent state of inferiority, or to defy the Government. We chose to defy the law. We first broke the law in a way which avoided any recourse to violence; when this form was legislated against, and when the Government resorted to a show of force to crush opposition to its policies, only then did we decide to answer violence with violence.

NELSON MANDELA (1918–)

The law in its majestic equality forbids the rich as well as the poor to sleep under bridges, to beg in the streets and to steal bread.

ANATOLE FRANCE (1844–1924)

What is the use of courts, if judges only quote authorities, and no judge exerts original jurisdiction, or recurs to first principles?

RALTH WALDO EMERSON
Address to the Citizens of Concord on the Fugitive Slave Law
(May 3, 1851)

Injustice anywhere is a threat to justice everywhere. We are caught in an inescapable network of mutuality, tied in a single garment of destiny. Whatever affects one directly, affects all indirectly.

MARTIN LUTHER KING, JR.
Letter from Birmingham Jail (1963)

"When the judge asks how you want to plead, say guilty . . .

And let the judge see that you notice what's going on."

"I hope Ma won't be there."

"I asked her to come. I want the judge to see her," Max said.

"She'll feel bad."

"All this is for you, Bigger."

"I reckon I ain't worth it."

"Well, this thing's bigger than you, son. In a certain sense, every Negro in America's on trial out there today."

RICHARD WRIGHT
Native Son (1940)

All the prosecution has been able to prove is that these boys wear long hair and zoot suits. All the rest has been circumstantial evidence, hearsay and war hysteria. The prosecution has tried to lead you to believe that they are some kind of inhuman gangsters. Yet they are Americans. Find them guilty of anything more serious than a juvenile bout of fisticuffs, and you will condemn all American youth. Find them guilty of murder, and you will murder the spirit of racial justice in America.

LUIS VALDEZ
Zoot Suit (1977)

One may ask: "How can you advocate breaking some laws and obeying others?" The answer lies in the fact that there are two types of laws: just and unjust. I would be the first to advocate obeying just laws. One has not only a legal but a moral responsibility to obey just laws. Conversely, one has a moral responsibility to disobey unjust laws. I would agree with St. Augustine that "an unjust law is no law at all."

MARTIN LUTHER KING, JR.
Letter from Birmingham Jail (1963)

But, setting aside the question of dishonor, there seems to be something wrong in petitioning a judge, and thus procuring an acquittal instead of informing and convincing him. For his duty is not to make a present of justice, but to give judgment; and he has sworn that he will judge according to the laws and not according to his own good pleaseure; and neither he nor we should get inot the habit of perjuring ourselves—there can be no piety in that.

PLATO
The Apology (c. 404 B.C.)

I am a slave, I know, and slaves are weak. But the gods are strong, and over them there stands some absolute, moral order or principle of law more final still. Upon this moral law the world depends; through it the gods exist; by it we live, defining good and evil. Apply that law to me. For if you flout it now, and those who murder in cold blood or defy the gods go unpunished, then human justice withers, corrupted at its source.

EURIPIDES
Hecuba (N.D.)

Meanwhile declining from the noon of day,
The sun obliquely shoots his burning ray;
The hungry judges soon the sentences sign,
And wretches hand that jurymen may dine.

ALEXANDER POPE
The Rape of the Lock (1714)

The ordinary human mind is a mass of prepossessions inherited and acquired, often, none the less dangerous because unrecognized by their possessors. Few minds are as neutral as a sheet of plate glass, and indeed a mind of that quality may actually fail in judicial efficiency, for the warmer tints of imagination and sympathy are needed to temper the old light of reason if human justice is to be done.

LORD MACMILLAN (1894–1986)

Though justice be thy plea, consider this,
That in the course of justice, none of us
Should see salvation: we do pray for mercy

WILLIAM SHAKESPEARE
The Merchant of Venice (1596)

Justice gazes most often into her literary mirror when she has been disheveled by the winds of social and political upheavel.

THEODORE ZIOLKOWSKI
The Mirror of Justice: Literary Reflections of Legal Crises (1997)

That Justice is a blind goddess
Is a thing to which we black are wise:
Her bandage hides two festering sores
That once perhaps were eyes.

LANGSTON HUGHES
"Justice" (1938)

Any law that uplifts human personality is just. Any law that degrades human personality is unjust. All segregation statutes are unjust because segregation distorts the soul and damages the personality.

MARTIN LUTHER KING, JR.
Letter from Birmingham Jail (1963)

The judges? The same judges who never intervened to save one life in seventeen years of dictatorship? Who never accepted a single habeas corpus? Judge Peralta who told that poor woman who had come to ask for her missing husband that that man had probably grown tired of her and run off with some other woman? That judge? What did you call him? A judge? A judge?

ARIEL DORFMAN
Death and the Maiden (1992)

Justice?—You get justice in the next world, in this world you have the law.

WILLIAM GADDIS
A Frolic of His Own (1994)

7

Cases and Judgments

Scarcely any political question arises in the United States that is not resolved, sooner or later, into a judicial question.

ALEXIS DE TOCQUEVILLE
Democracy in America (1835)

Who is to say that five men ten years ago were right whereas five men looking the other direction today are wrong?

U.S. SUPREME COURT JUSTICE HARRY A. BLACKMUN (1908–1999)
COMMENTING ON PRIOR COURT DECISIONS THAT ENDED IN 5-4 VOTES

Not in 124 years has a presidential election result been so disputed. Never in all those years have so many Americans believed that the winner of the White House actually lost the election. Nor in all of those years has the winning side been so convinced that the losing candidate was intent on "stealing the election."

E.J. DIONNE, JR. AND WILLIAM KRISTOL
from *Bush v. Gore* (2001)

He has blasphemed! Why do we still need witnesses?

CAIAPHAS, HIGH PRIEST,
AT THE TRIAL OF JESUS OF NAZARETH FOR BLASPHEMY AND HIGH
TREASON (33 A.D.)

"Jesus?" he replied, "Jesus, of Nazareth? No, I cannot
recall him to mind."

PONTIUS PILATE, LONG SINCE RETIRED, WHEN A FRIEND ASKS IF HE
REMEMBERS A CERTAIN TRIAL OVER WHICH HE HAD PRESIDED YEARS
BEFORE.

ANATOLE FRANCE
The Procurator of Judea (1896)

The unprecedented decision of the five justices to substitute their political judgment for that of the people threatens to undermine the moral authority of the high court for generations to come.

ALAN DERSHOWITZ
Supreme Injustice (2001)

From the beginning we've said we are going to respect the rule of law. If the Supreme Court of the United States says no more votes will be counted, then that's the end of it.

DAVID BOIES, ON NBC'S *Meet the Press* (2001)

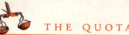

I offer my personal pledge to you and my family that I never again be involved in drugs or any illegality.

JOHN A. ZACCARO, JR. (AKA THE PHARMACIST), GERALDINE FERRARO'S SON, AT SENTENCING AFTER BEING CONVICTED OF SELLING COCAINE AT MIDDLEBURY COLLEGE

The sale of drugs was an insidious offense that demanded strong and firm measures.

JUDGE MCCAFFREY DURING THE TRIAL OF JOHN A. ZACCARO, JR. HE LATER SENTENCED ZACCARO TO HOUSE ARREST.

The public has a right to every man's evidence, except for those persons protected by a constitutional, common-law, or statutory privilege.

United States v. Bryan (1950)

Neither the doctrine of separation of powers, nor the need for confidentiality of high-level communications, without more, can sustain an absolute, unqualified Presidential privilege of immunity from judicial process under all circumstances.

U.S. CHIEF JUSTICE WARREN BURGER
United States v. Nixon (1974)

I am not a crook.

PRESIDENT RICHARD M. NIXON (1913–1994)

Gentlemen, judgment will not be passed on us by you; judgment will be passed on us by the Eternal Court of History . . . You may say "Guilty" a thousand times, but the Goddess who presides over the Eternal Court of History will, with a smile, tear up the indictment of the public prosecutor, and the verdict of this court, for she acquits us.

ADOLF HITLER, AFTER HIS TRIAL AND CONVICTION FOR TREASON (1924)

We believe that the decision of the Florida Supreme Court was correct, based on state law, and was a faithful and traditional application of this court's—of this state's statutes and precedents in dealing with election contests. And we believe when the Supreme Court ultimately hears this case, that will be their conclusion.

DAVID BOIES, REPRESENTING AL GORE IN
Bush v. Gore, QUOTED IN THE ASSOCIATED PRESS
(DECEMBER 10, 2000)

I bring out the worst in my enemies and that's how I get them to defeat themselves.

ROY COHN, QUOTED BY WILLIAM SAFIRE
IN *The New York Times* (AUGUST 4, 1986)

I think the law became an ass the day it let the psychiatrists get their hands on [it].

LYNN COMPTON, CHIEF DEPUTY DISTRICT ATTORNEY AT SIRHAN
SIRHAN'S TRIAL FOR THE ASSASSINATION OF ROBERT F. KENNEDY
(1968)

If you can manipulate news, a judge can manipulate the law. A smart lawyer can keep a killer out of jail, a smart accountant can keep a thief from paying taxes, a smart reporter could ruin your reputation—unfairly.

MARIO CUOMO (1932–)
FORMER GOVERNOR OF NEW YORK STATE

I hoped then that life might offer me the opportunity to serve my people and make my own humble contribution to their freedom struggle. This is what has motivated me in all that I have done in relation to the charges made against me in this case.

NELSON MANDELA (1918–)

If the glove doesn't fit, you must acquit.

JOHNNIE L. COCHRAN, JR. AT THE MURDER TRIAL OF O.J. SIMPSON (1994)

They can't change the law, they can't change the facts and they can't change the subject.

DAVID BOIES (1941–), THE GOVERNMENT'S LEAD ATTORNEY IN THE MICROSOFT ANTITRUST LAWSUIT

When you think of Napster, you think of music. But the first thing that struck me was that this was an important case not only for the music industry but for the whole of the Internet. . . this kind of noncommercial consumer copying is recognized as fair use under common-law theories and doctrines, and under the Supreme Court's criteria.

DAVID BOIES, DURING HIS *Wired* INTERVIEW (OCTOBER 2000), DISCUSSING THE NAPSTER CASE

Unless I am convinced by the testimony of the scriptures or by clear reason, I am bound by the scriptures I have quoted and my conscience is captive to the word of God. I cannot and will not retract anything. Here I stand, may God help me.

MARTIN LUTHER, AT HIS TRIAL FOR HERESY (1521)

With sincere heart and unfeigned faith I abjure, curse, and detest the above mentioned errors and heresies, and in general every other error, heresy, and sect contrary to the Holy Church.

GALILEO, AFTER HIS TRIAL AND CONVICTION FOR HERESY (1633)

Public opinion has its Bar as well as the Law Courts.

ANTHONY TROLLOPE
The Way We Live Now (1857)

Wherefore, O Judges, be of good cheer about death, and know this of a truth—that no evil can happen to a good man, either in life or after death . . . For which reason, also, I am not angry with my accusers or my condemners; they have done me no harm, although neither of them meant to do me any good; and for this I may gently blame them.

PLATO
The Apology (c. 404 B.C.)

Some of the things so far told to the court are true and some are untrue. I do not, however, deny that I planned sabotage. I did not plan it in a spirit of reck-lessness, nor because I have any love of violence. I planned it as a result of a calm and sober assessment of the political situation that had arisen after many years of tyranny, exploitation, and oppression of my people by the white.

NELSON MANDELA, AT THE RIVONA TRIAL (1964)

We think the right way to look at it is the way the four dissenting justices looked at it, which is that the legitimacy of any president that's elected is going to be impaired unless the American people understand that there has been a full and fair count of all the votes.

DAVID BOIES
Bush v. Gore (2001)

A suit could have brought as follows: "The Sabine property is mine." "No, it is mine." The trial should follow. But this was too simple for the lawyers. "A property which is situate in the district which is designated as Sabine." That is not bad enough, but look what follows: "This I affirm to be my property by Quiritary title." Then: "From this place I formally summon you to that place yonder to join issue with me according to law." Then the same lawyer goes over to the defendant's side, like a flute-playing accompanist: "From the place whence you have summoned me to join issue, from thence I summon you to that place yonder." The judge joins in: "The witnesses for both parties being there present, I formally indicate yonder road. Proceed on that road." Even our ancestors would have thought it ridiculous that men having hair duly presented themselves at a place should be told to leave it, only to return at once to the place from which they had gone.

CICERO (106–43 B.C.)

Precedent must bow to the general welfare—that is, when precedent is against us.

LOUIS AUCHINCLOSS
Diary of a Yuppie (1986)

I cannot in a moment refute great slanders; and, as I am convinced that I never wronged another, I will assuredly not wrong myself. I will not say of myself that I deserve any evil, or propose any penalty.

PLATO
The Apology (c. 404 B.C.)

Law and poetry arose together from the same bed.

JACOB GRIMM (1785–1863)

8

Freedom and Censorship

Let the word go forth from this time and place, to friend and foe alike, that the torch has been passed to a new generation of Americans . . . Let every nation know, whether it wishes us well or ill, that we shall pay any price, bear any burden, meet any hardship, support any friend, oppose any foe to assure the survival and the success of liberty.

PRESIDENT JOHN F. KENNEDY
INAUGURAL ADDRESS (1961)

We reaffirm that our constitutional command of free speech and assembly is fundamental and encompasses peaceful social protest.

JUSTICE ARTHUR GOLDBERG
Cox v. Louisiana (1965)

It is difficult to discern a serious threat to religious liberty from a room of silent, thoughtful schoolchildren.

U.S. SUPREME COURT JUSTICE SANDRA DAY O'CONNOR, CONCURRING OPINION IN A 6-3 RULING THAT AN ALABAMA LAW AUTHORIZING VOLUNTARY PRAYER OR MEDITATION IN PUBLIC SCHOOLS VIOLATED THE 1ST AMENDMENT BY ENCOURAGING RELIGIOUS PRACTICE (1985)

If a nation expects to be ignorant and free, in a state of civilization, it expects what never was and never will be.

PRESIDENT THOMAS JEFFERSON (1743–1826)

When the taste for physical pleasures has grown more rapidly than either education or experience of free institutions . . . there is no need to drag rights away from citizens . . . ; they themselves voluntarily let them go. They find it a tiresome inconvenience to exercise political rights which distract them from industry.

ALEXIS DE TOCQUEVILLE
Democracy in America (1835)

Give me the specifications and I'll give you the man . . . think of the possibilities. A society in which there is no failure, no boredom, no duplication of effort!

B. F. SKINNER
Walden Two (1948)

Men in their simplicity and their natural unruliness cannot even understand [freedom], they fear and dread it—for nothing has ever been more insupportable for a man and a human society than freedom.

THE GRAND INQUISITOR, IN FYODOR DOSTOEVSKY'S
The Brothers Karamazov (1879)

Students do not shed their constitutional rights to freedom of speech at the schoolhouse gates.

U.S. SUPREME COURT JUSTICE ABE FORTAS
Tinker v. Des Moines (1969)

We do not consecrate the flag by punishing its desecration, for in doing so we dilute the freedom that the cherished symbol represents.

U.S. SUPREME COURT JUSTICE WILLIAM J. BRENNAN, JR.
Texas v. Johnson (1989)

Protection, therefore, against the tyranny of the magistrate is not enough; there needs to be protection also against the tyranny of the prevailing opinion or feeling, against the tendency of society to impose, by other means than civil penalties, its own ideas and practices as rules of conduct on those who dissent from them.

JOHN STUART MILL
On Liberty (1859)

While I cannot take the time to name all of the men in the State Department who have been named as members of the Communist Party and members of a spy ring, I have here in my hand a list of 205 that were known to the secretary of state as being members of the Communist Party and who nevertheless are still working and shaping the policy of the State Department.

U.S. SENATOR JOSEPH MCCARTHY (1950)

I was not born to be forced. I will breathe after my own fashion.

HENRY DAVID THOREAU
Civil Disobedience (1849)

In my view it is unfortunate that some of my Brethren are apparently willing to hold that the publication of news may sometimes be enjoined. Such a holding would make a shambles of the First Amendment.

U.S. SUPREME COURT JUSTICE HUGO BLACK
DISSENTING OPINION IN *The New York Times v. United States* (1971)

We are a great nation, I think, largely because of our protection of the right to criticize, to dissent, to oppose, and to join with others in mass opposition—and to do these things powerfully and effectively.

U.S. SUPREME COURT JUSTICE ABE FORTAS (1910–1982)

[H]owever true it may be, if it is not fully, frequently, and fearlessly discussed, it will be held as a dead dogma, not a living truth.

JOHN STUART MILL
On Liberty (1859)

Before we begin dismantling constitutionally protected safeguards and diminishing fundamental rights to privacy, we should first examine why last week's attacks occurred.

CONGRESSMAN BOB BARR, R–GA (1948–)
THE WEEK AFTER SEPTEMBER 11, 2001

When there is war, the laws are silent.

CICERO (106–43B.C.)

Complete liberty of contradicting and disapproving our opinion is the very condition which justifies us in assuming its truth for purposes of action; and on no other terms can a being with human faculties have any rational assurance of being right.

JOHN STUART MILL
On Liberty (1859)

The important thing is not speaking one's own mind, but finding a way to have one's own mind.

ALLAN BLOOM
The Closing of the American Mind (1987)

Without the initiative that comes from immediate responsibility, ignorance will persist in the face of masses of information, however complete and correct.

JOSEPH A. SCHUMPETER (1883–1950)

If all mankind minus one were of one opinion, mankind would be no more justified in silencing that one person than he, if he had the power, would be justified in silencing mankind.

JOHN STUART MILL
On Liberty (1859)

Our civilization cannot afford to let the censor-moron loose. The censor-moron does not really hate anything but the living and growing human consciousness. It is our developing and extending consciousness that he threatens—and our consciousness in its newest, most sensitive activity, its vital growth. To arrest or circumscribe the vital consciousness is to produce morons, and nothing but a moron would do it.

D.H. LAWRENCE, WRITING IN
Sex, Literature and Censorship, EDITED BY HARRY T. MOORE
(1968)

We are aware now as then that it is dangerous to limit expression; and yet, without some limitations, civilization could not endure.

W. E. B. DuBois (1868–1963)

All errors which he is likely to commit against advice and warning are far outweighed by the evil of allowing others to constrain him to what they deem is good.

JOHN STUART MILL
On Liberty (1859)

We have no wish to offend with indecencies or obscenities, but we demand, as a right, the liberty to show the dark side of wrong that we may illuminate the bright side of virtue—the same liberty that is connected to the art of the written word—that art to which we owe the Bible and the works of Shakespeare.

D. W. GRIFFITH (1875–1948)

Every man—in the development of his own personality—has the right to form his own beliefs and opinions. Hence, suppression of belief, opinion, and expression is an affront to the dignity of man, a negation of man's essential nature.

THOMAS I. EMERSON
Toward a General Theory of the First Amendment (1963)

Compulsory unification of opinion achieves only the unanimity of the graveyard.

U.S. SUPREME COURT
West Virginia State Board of Education v. Barnette (1942)

Censorship is the strongest drive in human nature; sex is a weak second.

PHIL KERBY
Los Angeles Times

No one definition of obscenity, no matter how precisely or narrowly drawn, can possibly suffice for all situations, or carve out fully suppressible expression all media without also creating a substantial risk of encroachment upon the guarantees of the due process of the First Amendment.

U.S. SUPREME COURT JUSTICE WILLIAM J. BRENNAN, JR. (1906–1997)

I shall not today attempt further to define the kinds of materials I understand to be embraced within that shorthand definition; and perhaps I could never succeed in intelligibly doing so. But I know it when I see it, and the motion picture involved in this case is not that.

U.S. SUPREME COURT JUSTICE POTTER STEWART (1915–1985)

Sex and obscenity are not synonymous. Obscene material is material which deals with sex in a manner appealing to prurient interest. The portrayal of sex, e.g, in art, literature, and scientific works, is not itself sufficient reason to deny material the constitutional protection of freedom of speech and press. Sex, a great and mysterious motive force in human life, has indisputably been a subject of absorbing interest in mankind through the ages; it is one of the vital problems of human interest and public concern.

U.S. SUPREME COURT JUSTICE WILLIAM J. BRENNAN, JR. (1906–1997)

But when men have come to realize that time has upset many fighting faiths, they may come to believe even more than the foundations of their own conduct that the ultimate good desired is better reached by free trade in ideas—that the best test of truth is the power of the thought to get itself accepted in the competition of the market.

U.S. SUPREME COURT JUSTICE OLIVER WENDELL HOLMES, JR. (1841–1935)

Things economic and social move by their own momentum and the ensuing situations compel individuals and groups to behave in certain ways whatever they may wish to do—not indeed by destroying their freedom of choice but by shaping the choosing mentalities and by narrowing the list of possibilities from which to choose.

JOSEPH A. SCHUMPETER (1883–1950)

I am dead set against censorship. Especially when it emanates from special interest groups who have a highly special conception of what is moral. I have faith in the innate taste of all important film artists, and this taste has already been unmistakably displayed.

TENNESSEE WILLIAMS (1911–1983)

What New York has done . . . is to prevent the exhibition of a motion picture because that picture advocates an idea—that adultery under certain circumstances may be proper behavior. Yet the First Amendment's basic guarantee is of freedom to advocate ideas. The State, quite simply, has thus struck at the very heart of constitutionally protected liberty.

U.S. SUPREME COURT JUSTICE POTTER STEWART, DEFENDING *Lady Chatterley's Lover*

Those who won our independence believed that public discussion is a political duty and that this should be a fundamental principle of the American government. But they were confident people, not little men afraid of contrary ideas, afraid of criticism, afraid of public knowledge.

ANTHONY LEWIS, DEFENDING *If You Love This Planet,* AN ANTINUCLEAR DOCUMENTARY FILM, IN *The New York Times* (MARCH 3, 1983)

This is absolutely against public policy, against the spirit of the Constitution, against the very life and essence of what should be true American and democratic ideals. The mere fact of the races constituting the population of the U.S. are being shown in an unpleasant light is no argument whatever. If this factor is to be seriously considered, there is hardly any limit to which censorship may go.

LOUIS SHERWIN IN *The New York Globe*, DEFENDING D. W. GRIFFITH'S FILM *The Birth of a Nation* (1915)

There is no way to escape offending someone if you're writing about something important. But it's at the point where you cannot even do that. Nowadays, you cannot make a movie that says anything. It's reached a point of blandness.

OLIVER STONE (1946–)

The state has no legitimate interest in protecting any or all religions from views distasteful to them, which is sufficient to justify prior restraint upon the expression of those views. It is not the business of the givoverment in our nation to suppress real or imagined attacks upon a particular religious doctrine, whether they appear in publications, speeches, or motion pictures.

JUSTICE TOM C. CLARK (1899–1977)

All minorities have to allow for the possibility that there may be psychopaths or bad guys in their midst. Soon it will reach a point where the only villains you can put on the screen are WASP, straight males—and life is more complicated than that. It's a dangerous situation when artists can't engage honestly in the world because certain subjects are barred to them.

RICHARD SCHICKE (1947–)

We are not asking for censorship. We are asking Hollywood to use the same stystem of self-censorship they apply to other minorities. Nobody would dare to do a film about a group of organized black men whose objective is to rape a white woman. We always find ourselves in a position of having to play civil libertarian to a bunch of bigots who want their constitutional right to express their hatred of us.

Ronald Gold, media advisor for the National Gay Task Force, defending the movie *Cruising* (1980)

It is a crime to poison the minds of the little and the humble, to exasperate the passions of reaction and intolerance, while seeking refuge behind that odious anti-Semitism of which great liberal France, France of the rights of man, will die, unless she is cured of her disease. It is a crime to exploit patriotism for works of hatred, and, finally, it is a crime to make of the sword a modern God when all human science is labouring for the coming work of truth and justice.

EMILE ZOLA
"J'Accuse" (1898)

We are not talking about censorship here, we're talking about balance. We had 2,000 years of one message. We want to have parity.

TOM AMANIANO, GAY AND LESBIAN ALLIANCE AGAINST DEFAMATION, ON THE SEX-ABUSE SCANDAL IN THE CATHOLIC CHURCH (2002)

Thomas: It is very apparent that you are following the same line of these other witnesses.

Bessie: I am following no line—.

Thomas: Which is definitely the Communist line.

Bessie: I am using my own head, which I am privileged to do.

Thomas: You are excused. If you want to make a speech, go out there under a big tree.

ALVAH BESSIE, BEFORE THE HOUSE UN-AMERICAN ACTIVITIES COMMITTEE, FROM *Inquisition in Eden* (1965)

9

Crime and Punishment

We assert that flogging in the navy is opposed to the essential dignity of man, which no legislator has the right to violate; that it is oppressive, and glaringly unequal in its operations; that it is utterly repugnant to the spirit of our democratic institutions; indeed that it involves a lingering trait of the worst times of a barbarous feudal aristocracy; in a word we denounce it as religiously, morally, and immutably wrong.

HERMAN MELVILLE
White-Jacket (1851)

Zaccaro is a drug felon and he's living in conditions that 99.9% of the people of Vermont couldn't afford.

JOHN QUINN, THE ADDISON COUNTY STATE'S ATTORNEY
WHO PROSECUTED JOHN ZACCARO, JR. (1986)

You tell me you are my judge. Ponder with great care what you mean to do, for in very truth I was sent of God, and you are putting yourself in great jeopardy.

JOAN OF ARC AT HER TRIAL IN ROUEN, FRANCE (JANUARY 9, 1431)

I never took a decision by myself. I never did anything, great or small, without obtaining advance express instructions from my superiors.

ADOLF EICHMANN, AT HIS WAR-CRIMES TRIAL IN ISRAEL FOR PLANNING AND EXECUTING THE NAZI HOLOCAUST. HE WAS CONVICTED AND HANGED. (1961)

The responsibility of a public prosecutor differs from that of the usual advocate; it is to seek justice, not merely to convict.

THE NEW YORK STATE BAR ASSOCIATION
The Lawyer's Code of Professional Responsibility (1999)

DNA tests have cleared more than 1,000 people who have spent a total of more than 3,000 years in prison for crimes they did not commit.

RECENT REVELATION

I decided to take, in every predicament, the victim's side, so as to reduce the damage done.

ALBERT CAMUS
The Plague (1957)

A person may cause evil to others not only by his actions but by his inaction, and in either case he is justly accountable to them for the injury.

JOHN STUART MILL
On Liberty (1859)

A public prosecutor or other government lawyer shall not institute or cause to be instituted when he or she knows or it is obvious that the charges are not supported by probable cause.

THE NEW YORK STATE BAR ASSOCIATION
The Lawyer's Code of Professional Responsibility (1999)

Wrong must not win by technicalities.

AESCHYLUS (?–456 B.C.)
The Eumenides (N.D.), TRANSLATED BY RICHMOND LATTIMORE

. . . you don't have many suspects who are innocent.

U.S. ATTORNEY GENERAL EDWIN MEESE III (1931–), WHO SERVED
UNDER PRESIDENT RONALD REAGAN, DENOUNCING "THE RIGHT TO
REMAIN SILENT."

He must be warned prior to any questioning that he has the right to remain silent, that anything he says can be used against him in a court of law, that he has the right to the presence of an attorney, and that if he cannot afford an attorney one will be appointed for him prior to any questioning if he so desires.

U.S. CHIEF JUSTICE EARL WARREN
Miranda v. Arizona (1966)

Can we not convict and yet mitigate the penalty?

HERMAN MELVILLE
Billy Budd (1924)

Seldom does the degree of probability suggested by evidence lend itself readily to mathematical expression or attain numeric precision.

CHRISTOPHER MUELLER AND LAIRD KIRKPATRICK
Evidence Under the Rules (N.D.)

Mistrust of juries is the single overriding reason for the law of evidence.

ANONYMOUS

No person shall be compelled in any criminal case to be a witness against himself.

THE FIFTH AMENDMENT TO THE UNITED STATES CONSTITUTION

Silence is at least not denial, and may be consent.

HERMAN MELVILLE
The Confidence Man (1852)

It is better to risk saving a guilty person than to condemn an innocent one.

VOLTAIRE (1694–1778)

It is better that ten guilty persons escape than one innocent suffer.

SIR WILLIAM BLACKSTONE (1723–1780)

Rules of evidence and procedure are designed to lead to just decisions and are part of the framework of the law.

THE NEW YORK STATE BAR ASSOCIATION
The Lawyer's Code of Professional Responsibility (1999)

"Do you affirm that the treasonous officer was Captain Dreyfus?"
"I swear to it."

MAJOR HUBERT HENRY, PERJURING HIMSELF AT THE TRIAL FOR TREASON OF CAPTAIN ALFRED DREYFUS IN PARIS (1894). DREYFUS WAS CONVICTED, BUT LATER ACQUITTED AFTER AN APPEAL, AND AFTER SERVING TIME ON DEVIL'S ISLAND, FRENCH GUIANA.

The most beautiful words in the English language are "not guilty."

MAXIM GORKY (1868–1936)

When dealing with a legal matter—always remember that you are your own best advocate. No one will care as much about the case as you do. Use lawyers but remember—you must take primary responsibility for a successful outcome.

GRANT FAIRLEY (1958–)

Litigation takes the place of sex at middle age.

GORE VIDAL (1925–)

There are two kinds of lawyers, those who know the law and those who know the judge.

ANONYMOUS

Certain crimes seem to epitomize the thinking of their era.

MEYER LEVIN
Compulsion (1956)

I'm no idealist to believe firmly in the integrity of our courts and in the jury system—that is no ideal to me, it is a living, working reality. Gentlemen, a court is no better than each man of you sitting before me on this jury. A court is only as sound as its jury, and a jury is only as sound as the men who make it up.

HARPER LEE
To Kill a Mockingbird (1960)

The Court: "What evidence do you have that you want to present?"

Mr. Gilmore: "Apparently I don't have any, according to my lawyers"

NORMAN MAILER
The Executioner's Song (1990)

Mr. Savage tells the court that if these boys are hanged there will be no more boys like these.

CLARENCE DARROW, PLEADING FOR MERCY FOR NATHAN LEOPOLD
AND RICHARD LOEB (1924)

What debt did she owe to a social order which had condemned and banished her without a trial? She had never been heard in her own defence; she was innocent of the charge on which she had been found guilty . . .

LILY BART, CHARACTER IN EDITH WHARTON'S
The House of Mirth (1905)

Gentlemen of the jury, who would be hurt if you took this life? Look back to that second row. Please look. I want all twelve of you honorable men to turn your heads and look back to that second row. What you see there has been everything to him—mama, grandmother, godmother—everything. Look at her, gentlemen of the jury, look at her well. Take this away from her, and she has no reason to go on living. We may see him as not much, but he's her reason for existence. Think on that, gentlemen, think on it.

ERNEST GAINES
A Lesson Before Dying (1993)

Ah, should you lose at last, yet you and he,
Each in the certitude the other gave,
Strong in your love, and by your love made free,
Would bear some goodness to the utter grave!

YVOR WINTERS (1900–1968),

To a Woman on Her Defense of Her Brother Unjustly Convicted of Murder: Written after an Initial Study of the Evidence

What Rufus needed more than anything else was a big, nasty, controversial, well-publicized conviction in a murder trial.

> JOHN GRISHAM
> *A Time to Kill* (1987)

Saving face is one of the most important and least spoken "defenses" known to criminal law.

> ROBERT TRAVER
> *Anatomy of a Murder* (1958)

"Citizen President," the accused Rubashov declared, "I speak here for the last time in my life. The opposition is beaten and destroyed. If I ask myself to-day, 'For what am I dying?' I am confronted by absolute nothingness. There is nothing for which one could die, if one died without having repented and unreconciled with the Party and the Movement. Therefore, on the threshold of my last hour, I bend my knees to the country, to the masses and to the whole people."

ARTHUR KOESTLER
Darkness at Noon (1940)

The quality of mercy is not strain'd. It droppeth as a gentle rain from heaven upon the places beneath. It is an attribute to God himself, and earthly power doth then show likest God's, when mercy seasons justice.

WILLIAM SHAKESPEARE
The Merchant of Venice (1596)

We're going to put him on trial, Gerado, this doctor. Right here. Today. You and me. Or is your famous investigating Commission going to do it?

ARIEL DORFMAN
Death and the Maiden (1992)

The twofold aim of criminal justice is that guilt shall not escape or innocence suffer.

BERGER V. UNITED STATES (1935)

10

At the Expense of Lawyers: Quips, Jokes, and Scandalous Sayings

All sides in a lawsuit want to hide at least some of the truth.

ALAN M. DERSHOWITZ (1938–)
PROFESSOR, HARVARD LAW SCHOOL

The movies are the only court where the judge goes to the lawyer for advice.

F. SCOTT FITZGERALD
The Crack-Up (1945)

The startling thing is that lawyers don't seem to like to laugh at themselves, or even get mildly amused about their profession.

ANN SLEEPER, IN *Roth and Roth, Devil's Advocates: The Unnatural History of Lawyers* (1989)

It seems to me that there must be an ecological limit to the number of paper pushers the earth can sustain, and that human civilization will collapse when the number of, say, tax lawyers exceeds the world's total population of farmers, weavers, fisherpersons, and pediatric nurses.

BARBARA EHRENREICH, QUOTED IN *Ms.* MAGAZINE (1986)

There is a rhythm to the ending of a marriage just like the rhythm of a courtship—only backward. You try to start again but get into blaming over and over. Finally you are both worn out, exhausted, hopeless. Then lawyers are called in to pick clean the corpses. The death has occurred much earlier.

ERICA JONG
How to Save Your Own Life (1977)

He saw a lawyer killing a viper on a dunghill hard by
    his own stable
And the Devil smiled, for it put him in mind of Cain
    and his brother Abel.

SAMUEL TAYLOR COLERIDGE (1772–1834)

I was never ruined but twice — once when I lost a lawsuit, and once when I gained one.

VOLTAIRE (1694–1778)

The only thing a lawyer won't question is the legitimacy of his mother.

W. C. FIELDS (1879–1946)

A lawyer is one who defends you at the risk of your pocketbook, reputation and life.

EUGENE E. BRUSSELL (1947–)

The other day my house caught fire. My lawyer said, "Shouldn't be a problem. What kind of coverage do you have?" I said, "Fire and theft." The lawyer frowned. "Uh-oh. Wrong kind. Should be fire or theft."

ALAN KING (1927–)

———

A lawyer is a chimney-sweeper who has no objection to dirty work, because it is his trade.

CHARLES CALEB COLTON (1780–1832)

Where there is a rift in the lute, the business of the lawyer is to widen the rift and gather the loot.

ARTHUR G. HAYS (1884–1954)

I think we may class the lawyer in the natural history of monsters.

JOHN KEATS (1795–1821)

A lawyer's dream of Heaven: Every man reclaimed his own property at the resurrection, and each tried to recover it from all his forefathers.

SAMUEL BUTLER (1835–1902)

I'll never forget my father's response when I told him I wanted to be a lawyer. He said, "If you do this, no man will ever want you."

CASSANDRA DUNN (1931–)

When one wanted one's interests looked after whatever the cost, it was not so well for a lawyer to be over honest, else he might not be up to other people's tricks.

George Eliot (*pseudonym of* Mary Ann Evans) (1819–1880)

God works wonders now and then: Behold, a lawyer, an honest man.

Benjamin Franklin (1706–1790)

Lawyers spend a great deal of their time shoveling smoke.

U.S. SUPREME COURT JUSTICE OLIVER WENDELL HOLMES, JR.
(1841–1935)

A lawyer is a person who writes a 10,000-word document and calls it a "brief."

FRANZ KAFKA (1883–1924)

For example, if my neighbor hath a mind to my cow, he hires a lawyer to prove that he ought to have my cow from me. I must then hire a lawyer to defend my right . . . My lawyer, being practiced almost from his cradle in defending falsehood, is quite out of his element when he would be an advocate for justice, which as an office unnatural, he always attempts with great awkwardness, if not ill-will . . .

JONATHAN SWIFT
Gulliver's Travels (1726)

In London it is against the law to fall asleep on a bus; a London bus company recently prosecuted a nun whose ticket had become invalid after she fell asleep and missed her stop.

DAVID CROMBIE
The World's Stupidest Laws (2000)

———

Death is not the end. There remains the litigation over the estate.

AMBROSE BIERCE (1842–1914)

Lawyers are like rhinoceroses: thick skinned, short-sighted, and always ready to charge.

DAVID MELLOR (1949–)
BRITISH CONSERVATIVE POLITICIAN

We do not get good laws to restrain bad people. We get good people to restrain bad laws.

G. K. CHESTERTON
All Things Considered (1909)

A lawyer will do anything to win a case, sometimes he will even tell the truth.

PATRICK MURRAY (1959–)

In university they don't tell you that the greater part of the law is learning to tolerate fools.

DORIS LESSING (1919–)

You're an attorney. It's your duty to lie, conceal and distort everything, and slander everybody.

JEAN GIRAUDOUX
The Madwoman of Chaillot (1945)

It was so cold in Montana that the lawyers had their hands in their own pockets.

DAVID CROMBIE
The World's Stupidest Laws (2000)

litigant n. A person about to give up his skin for the hope of retaining his bones.

AMBROSE BIERCE
The Devil's Dictionary (1908)

The average lawyer is essentially a mechanic who works with a pen instead of a ball peen hammer.

ROBERT SCHMITT
Americans for Legal Reform Newsletter (1984)

Talk is cheap. . . until lawyers get involved.

ANONYMOUS

The devil hates a civil lawyer, as a soldier does peace.

THOMAS DEKKER
The Virgin Martir, III, iii (1622)

Lawyers, like painters, can easily change white into black.

AMERICAN PROVERB

Being divorced is like being hit by a Mack truck—if you survive you start looking very carefully to the right and left.

JEAN KERR
Mary, Mary (1963)

The first thing we do, let's kill all the lawyers.

WILLIAM SHAKESPEARE
The Life of Henry V, Part 2 (1599)

———

Sometimes I think we're the only two lawyers in Washington who trust each other.

ELIZABETH DOLE, SPEAKING TO HER HUSBAND, SENATOR BOB DOLE
QUOTED IN *Newsweek* (AUGUST 3, 1987)

People are getting smarter nowadays; they are letting lawyers, instead of their conscience, be their guide.

WILL ROGERS (1879–1935)

I don't want to know what the law is, I want to know who the judge is.

ROY COHN (1927–1986)

It is the trade of lawyers to question everything, yield nothing, and to talk by the hour.

PRESIDENT THOMAS JEFFERSON (1743–1826)

I have come to the conclusion that one useless man is called a disgrace, two men are called a law firm, and three or more become a Congress.

PRESIDENT JOHN ADAMS, IN HIS PLAY 1776

In the Halls of Justice the only justice is in the halls.

LENNY BRUCE (1925–1966)

My daddy is a movie actor, and sometimes he plays the good guy, and sometimes he plays the lawyer.

MALCOLM FORD, TO HIS PRESCHOOL CLASSMATES ON WHAT HIS
FATHER, ACTOR HARRISON FORD, DOES FOR A LIVING.

My parents wanted me to be a lawyer. But I don't think I would have been very happy. I'd be in front of the jury singing.

JENNIFER LOPEZ (1970–)

I began wearing hats as a young lawyer because it helped me to establish my professional identity. Before that, whenever I was at a meeting, someone would ask me to get coffee.

BELLA ABZUG (1920–1998)

---

lawsuit n. a machine which you go into as a pig and come out as a sausage.

AMBROSE BIERCE
The Devils Dictionary (1908)

---

lawyer n. One skilled in circumvention of the law.

AMBROSE BIERCE
The Devil's Dictionary (1908)

The Judges are Going to Jail
Hurrah for the masses,
The lawyers are asses,
Their gammon and spinach is stale!
The law is illegal
The Commons are regal,
And the Judges are going to jail.
Hurrah for the masses.
The lawyers are asses
The Judges are going to jail.

ANONYMOUS (C. 1860)

I know you lawyers can with ease
Twist words and meanings as you please;
That language, by your skill made pliant,
Will bend, to favor every client;
That 'tis the fee limits the sense
To make out either side's pretense,
When you peruse the clearest case,
You see it with a double face,
For skepticism's your profession,
You hold there's doubt it all expression.

BENJAMIN FRANKLIN (1706–1790)
"POOR RICHARD'S OPINION"

LAW is an artistically valuable (i.e. intrinsic, senti-ment-dependent, intersubjective, anthropocentric, incommensurable, contextual, contingent, non-ethno-centric, objective) action type (i.e. performance achieved by the artist, possessed of structure and heuristic, capable of multiple instantiation).

GARY BAGNALL
Law as Art (1996)

The rich attorney was good as his word;
The briefs came trooping gaily,
And every day my voice was heard
At the Sessions of Ancient Bailey.
All thieves who could my fees afford
Relied on my orations,
And many a burglar I've restored
To his friends and his relations.

W.S. GILBERT AND ARTHUR SULLIVAN
Trial by Jury (1875)

Hark, the hour of ten is sounding:
Hearts with anxious fears are bounding,
Hall of Justice crowds surrounding,
    Breathing hope and fear—
For to-day in this arena,
Summoned by a stern subpoena,
Edwin, sued by Angelina,
    Shortly will appear.

W.S. Gilbert and Arthur Sullivan
Trial by Jury (1875)

In law, what pleas so tainted and corrupt,
But being seasoned with a gracious voice,
Obscures the show of evil.

WILLIAM SHAKESPEARE
The Merchant of Venice (1596)

If half the lawyers would become plumbers, two of man's biggest problems would be solved.

FELTON DAVIS, JR.
"Reflections on the Lake" (1986)

When the lawyers are through
What is there left, Bob?
Can a mouse nibble at it
And find enough to fasten a tooth in?

CARL SANDBURG (1878-1967)
"The Lawyers Know Too Much"

Going to trial with a lawyer who considers your whole life-style a crime in progress is not a happy prospect.

HUNTER S. THOMPSON (1939–)

Contributors

A

Abzug, Bella (1920–1998)
Adams, Abigail (b. Smith) (1744–1818)
Adams, George (1910–)
Adams, John (1735–1826)
Aeschylus (?–456 B.C.)
Aleichem, Sholem (*pseudonym of* Solomon J. Rabinowitz)
    (1859–1916)
Alexie, Sherman (1966–)
Anouilh, Jean (1910–1987)
Aristotle (384–322 B.C.)
Auchincloss, Louis (1917–)
Auden, W. H. (Wystan Hugh) (1907–1973)
Augustine, St. (also known as Augustine of Canterbury) (? –604)

B

Bagnall, Gary (1959–)
Barr, Bob (1948–)
Barth, John (1930–)
Beecher, Henry Ward (1813–1887)

Beecher Stowe, Harriet (Elizabeth) (1811–1896)
Belli, Melvin M. (1907–1996)
Bender, George Harrison ("Harry") (1896–1961)
Bentham, Jeremy (1748–1832)
Bessie, Alvah (1904–1985)
Bierce, Ambrose (1842–1914)
Black, Hugo (1886–1971)
Blackmun, Harry A. (1908–1999)
Blackstone, Sir William (1723–1780)
Blake, William (1757–1827)
Bloom, Allan (1930–1992)
Boies, David (1941–)
Boswell, James (1740–1795)
Brecht, (Eugene) Bertolt (Friedrich) (1898–1956)
Brennan, William J. Jr. (1906–1997)
Bruce, Lenny (1925–1966)
Brussell, Eugene E. (1947–)
Burger, Warren (1907–1995)
Bush, George W. (1946–)
Butler, Samuel (1835–1902)

C

Caesar (*in full* Gaius Julius Caesar DT) (101–44 B.C.)
Camus, Albert (1913–1960)
Cannon, Lou (1938–)

Capote, Truman (1924–1984)
Cardozo, Benjamin (Nathan) (1870–1938)
Carver, Robert (1967–)
Cervantes (Saavedra), Miguel de (1547–1616)
Chesterton, G.K. (1874–1936)
Choate, Rufus (1799–1859)
Chomsky, Noam (1928–)
Cicero (106–43 B.C.)
Clark, Tom C. (1899–1977)
Cochran, Johnnie Jr. (1937–)
Cohn, Roy (1927–1986)
Cole, George F. (1935–)
Coleridge, Samuel Taylor (1772–1834)
Colton, Charles Caleb (1780–1832)
Compton, Lynn (1937–)
Cooper, James Fenimore (1789–1851)
Cox, Archibald (1912–)
Crane, Frank (1861–1928)
Crombie, David (1949–)
Cuomo, Mario (1932–)

D
Darrow, Clarence (1857–1938)
Davis, Felton, Jr. (1942–)
Dekker, Thomas (?–1641)

Dershowitz, Alan M. (1938–)
Dickens, Charles (1812–1870)
Diderot, Denis (1713–1784)
Disraeli, Benjamin (1804–1881)
Dole, Elizabeth (1936–)
Dorfman, Ariel (1942–)
Dostoevsky, Fyodor (1821–1881)
Douglas, William O. (1898–1980)
Dreyfus, Alfred (1859 –1935)
DuBois, W.E.B. (William Edward Burghardt) (1868–1963)
Dunn, Cassandra (1931–)

E

Ehrenreich, Barbara (1941–)
Eichmann, Adolf (1906–1962)
Eisenhower, Dwight D. (1890–1969)
Eliot, George (*pseudonym of* Mary Ann Evans) (1819–1880)
Emerson, Ralph Waldo (1803–1882)
Emerson, Thomas I. (1938–)
Euripides (? 480–406 B.C.)

F

Fairley, Grant (1958–)
Faulkner, William (1897–1962)
Fields, W.C. (1879–1946)

Fitzgerald, F. Scott (1896–1940)

Ford, Malcolm (1987–)

Fortas, Abe (1910–1982)

Fortescue, Lord Chief Justice (?1698–?)

France, Anatole (*pseudonym of* Jacques Anatole François Thibault)
    (1844–1924)

Frankfurter, Felix (1882–1965)

Franklin, Benjamin (1706–1790)

Freedman, James O. (1936–)

French, Marilyn (1929–)

Fuller, Thomas (1654–1734)

G

Gaddis, William (1922–1998)

Gaines, Ernest (1933–)

Galileo (1564–1642)

Galsworthy, John (1867–1933)

Gandhi, Mohandas K. (1869–1948)

Gates, Henry Louis, Jr. (1950–)

Gay, John (1685–1732)

George, Ronald (1940–)

Gilbert, W.S. (1836–1911)

Ginsburg, Ruth Bader (1933–)

Giraudoux, Jean (1882–1944)

Gladstone, William (1809–1898)

Glover, Jonathan (1943–)
Goldberg, Arthur (1908–1990)
Goldman, Robert (1947–)
Gorky, Maxim (1868–1936)
Goldsmith, Oliver (1728–1774)
Goss, Porter J. (1938–)
Grant, Ulysses S. (1822–1885)
Griffith, D.W. (1875–1948)
Grimm, Jacob (1785–1863)
Grimm, Wilhelm (1786–1859)
Grisham, John (1955–)

H

Hamilton, Alexander (1757–1804)
Hand, Learned (1872–1961)
Harlan, John Marshall (1899–1971)
Harrington, Michael (1928-1989)
Hawthorne, Nathaniel (1804–1864)
Hays, Arthur G. (1884–1954)
Hellman, Lillian (1905–1984)
Hemingway, Ernest (1899–1961)
Hesse, Hermann (1877–1962)
Higgins, George V. (1939–1999)
Hitler, Adolf (1889–1945)
Holmes, Oliver Wendell Jr. (1841–1935)

Homer (c. 850 B.C.–?)
Houston, Charles H. (1895–1950)
Hughes, Charles Evans (1862–1948)
Hughes, Langston (1902–1967)
Humphrey, Hubert (1911–1978)

I

Iacocca, Lee (1924–)

J

Jackson, Andrew (1767–1845)
Jay, John (1745–1829)
Jefferson, Thomas (1743–1826)
Joan of Arc (1412–1431)
Johnson, Earl Jr. (1934–)
Johnson, Lyndon B. (1908–1973)
Jong, Erica (1942–)

K

Kafka, Franz (1883–1924)
Kallen, Lucille (1922–1999)
Kaufman, Irving (1910–1992)
Keats, John (1795–1821)
Kennedy, John Fitzgerald (1917–1963)
Kennedy, Robert Francis (1925–1968)

Kent, James (Chancellor) (1763–1847)
Kerby, Phil (1957–)
Kerr, Jean (1923–)
King, Alan (1927–)
King, Martin Luther, Jr. (1929–1968)
Koestler, Arthur (1905–1983)

L

Lamb, Charles (1775–1834) (*pseudonym* Elia)
Lawrence, D.H. (1885–1930)
Lessing, Doris (1919–)
Levin, Meyer (N.D.)
Lewis, Anthony (1936–)
Lincoln, Abraham (1809–1865)
Lopez, Jennifer (1970–)
Luther, Martin (1483–1546)

M

MacMillan, Lord (1894–1986)
Mailer, Norman (1923–)
Mandela, Nelson (Rolihlahla) (1918–)
Mansfield, Lord (1697–1762)
Marshall, John (1755–1835)
Marshall, Thurgood (1908–1993)
McCarthy, Joseph (1909–1957)

Meese, Edwin, III (1931–)
Mellor, David (1949–)
Melville, Herman (1819–1891)
Mill, John Stuart (1806–1873)
Moore, Hoyt A. (1874–1969)
More, Sir Thomas (also St. Thomas More) (1478–1535)
Morgan, J. Pierpont (1837–1913)
Murray, Patrick (N.D.)
William Murray (Lord Mansfield) (1705–1793)

N
Nagel, Thomas (1937–)
The New York State Bar Association
Nixon, Richard M. (1913–1994)

O
Oaks, Dallin H. (1932–)
O'Connor, Sandra Day (1930–)
O'Neil, Paul (1952–)
Osborne, John J. (1929–1994)

P
Packard, Edward Jr. (1951–)
Paine, Thomas (1737–1809)
Parks, Rosa (1913–)

Pascal, Blaise (1623–1662)
Phenix, Philip H. (1915–2002)
Pirsig, Robert M. (1928–)
Pitt, William (1759–1806)
Plato (? 427–347 B.C.)
Pope, Alexander (1688–1744)
Powell, Adam Clayton, Jr. (1908–1972)
Powell, Lewis Jr. (1907–)
Prosser, William Lloyd (1898–)

Q

Quinn, Jane Bryant (1946–)
Quinn, John (1951–)

R

Reno, Janet (1938–)
Roby, Pamela (1961–)
Rogers, Will (1879–1935)
Roosevelt, Theodore (1858–1919)
Rousseau, Jean Jacques (1712–1778)
de Rouvroy, Claude Henri (Comte de Saint-Simon) (1760–1825)
Rutledge, Wiley Blount, Jr. (1894–1949)

S

Sallust (*in full* Gaius Sallustius Crispus) (86–34 B.C.)

Sandburg, Carl (1878–1967)

Schicke, Richard (1947–)

Schumpeter, Joseph A. (1883–1950)

Shakespeare, William (1564-1616)

Shapiro, Irving S. (1916–2001)

Shaw, Lemuel (1781–1861)
(Massachusetts Supreme Court Chief Justice)

Sherwin, Lewis (N.D.)

Silberman, Lawrence (1935–)

Silone, Ignazio (*pseudonym* of Secondo Tranquilli) (1900–1978)

Skinner, B.F. (1904–1980)

Sleeper, Ann (N.D.)

Smith, Carl (N.D.)

Stead, Christina (1902–1983)

Stewart, Potter (1915–1985)

Stone, Oliver (1946–)

Story, Joseph (1779–1845)

Streisand, Barbra (1942–)

Sturgess (Judge) (N.D.)

Sullivan, Arthur (1842–1900)

Swift, Jonathan (1667–1745)

T

Taffel, Ron (1942–)

Taft, William Howard (1857–1930)

Theophrastus (372–286 B.C.)
Thomas, Clarence (1948–)
Thompson, E.P. (1924–1993)
Thompson, Hunter S. (1939–)
Thoreau, Henry David (1817–1862)
de Tocqueville, Alexis (1805–1859)
Train, Arthur C. (1875–1945)
Traver, Robert (*pseudonym* of John D. Voelker) (1903–1991)
Trevor, Claire (1909–2000)
Trollope, Anthony (1815–1882)
Twain, Mark (1835–1910)

V
Valdez, Luis (1940–)
Vidal, Gore (1925–)
Voltaire (*pseudonym* of Jean-Marie Arouet) (1694–1778)

W
Walker, Alice (1944–)
Warren, Earl (1891–1974)
Webster, Daniel (1782–1852)
Wharton, Edith (1862–1937)
White, James Boyd (1939–)
Whitehead, Alfred North (1861–1947)
Whitehead, Ted (1900–1967)

Wilde, Oscar (1854–1900)
Williams, Tennessee (1911–1983)
Wilson, (Thomas) Woodrow (1856–1924)
Winters, Yvor (1900–1968)
Wolfe, Tom (1931–)
Wright, Richard (1908–1960)

Z
Zaccaro, John A. Jr. (1966–)
Ziolkowski, Theodore (1932–)
Zola, Emile (1840–1902)

Works Cited

A

Alexie, Sherman (1966–)
At the Trial of Hamlet (1994)

Anouilh, Jean (1910–1987)
Antigone (1939)

Auchincloss, Louis (1917–)
Diary of a Yuppie (1986)

Auden, W. H. (Wystan Hugh) (1907–1973)
"A Law Like Love" (1939)

B

Bagnall, Gary
Law as Art (1996)

Barth, John (1930–)
The Floating Opera (N.D.)

Beecher, Henry Ward (1813–1887)
Proverbs from Plymouth Pulpit (1847)

Beecher Stowe, Harriet (Elizabeth) (1811–1896)
Uncle Tom's Cabin (1852)

Bessie, Alvah (1904–1985)
Inquisition in Eden (1965)

Blake, William (1757–1827)
"The Marriage of Heaven and Hell" (1794)

Bloom, Allan (1930–1992)
The Closing of the American Mind (1987)

Brecht, (Eugene) Bertolt (Friedrich) (1898–1956)
The Threepenny Opera (1928)

C

Camus, Albert (1913–1960)
The Plague (1957)

Capote, Truman (1924–1984)
In Cold Blood (1966)

Cardozo, Benjamin (Nathan) (1870–1938)
Law and Literature and Other Essays (1931)

Cervantes (Saavedra), Miguel de (1547–1616)
Don Quixote (1604)

Chesterton, G.K. (1874–1936)
All Things Considered (1909)

Cole, George F. (1935–)
The American System of Criminal Justice (2000)

Crombie, David (1949–)
The World's Stupidest Laws (2000)

D

Davis, Felton Jr. (N.D.)
"Reflections on the Lake", *The Gainesville Times* (GA)

Dershowitz, Alan M. (1938–)
Supreme Injustice (2001)

Dickens, Charles (1812–1870)
Bleak House (1853)
Little Dorrit (1857)
Great Expectations (1861)

Dorfman, Ariel (1942–)
Death and the Maiden (1992)

Dostoevsky, Fyodor (1821–1881)
The Brothers Karamazov (1879)

E
Emerson, Ralph Waldo (1803–1882)
Address to the Citizens of Concord on the Fugitive Slave Law
(May 3, 1851)

Emerson, Thomas I. (1927–)
Toward a General Theory of the First Amendment (1963)

Euripides (? 480–406 B.C.)
Hecuba (N.D.)

F
Faulkner, William (1897–1962)
Sartoris (1929)
Knight's Gambit (1949)
Essays (1960)

Fitzgerald, F. Scott (1896–1940)
The Crack-Up (1945)

France, Anatole (1844–1924)
The Procurator of Judea (1896)

French, Marilyn (1929–)
Beyond Power: On Women, Men and Morals (1986)

Fuller, Thomas (1654–1734)
Gnomologia (1732)

G

Gaddis, William (1922–1998)
A Frolic of his Own (1994)

Gaines, Ernest (1933–)
A Lesson Before Dying (1993)

Gates, Henry Louis, Jr. (1950–)
Colored People (1995)

Gilbert, W.S. (1836–1911) and Sullivan, Arthur (1842–1900)
Trial by Jury (1875)

Giraudoux, Jean (1882–1944)
The Madwoman of Chaillot (*La Folle de Chaillot*) (1943)

Glover, Jonathan (1943–)
Causing Death and Saving Lives (1977)

Goldman, Robert (1947–)
The Modern Art of Cross-Examination (1993)

Griffith, D.W. (1875–1948)
film *The Birth of a Nation* (1915)

Grisham, John (1955–)
A Time to Kill (1987)
The Firm (1991)
The Client (1993)
The Rainmaker (1995)

H

Harrington, Michael (1928–1989)
The Other America: Poverty in the United States (1962)

Hawthorne, Nathaniel (1804–1864)
The Scarlet Letter (1850)

Hemingway, Ernest (1899–1961)
The Old Man and the Sea (1952)

Hesse, Hermann (1877–1962)
Demian (1919)

Higgins, George V. (1939–1999)
Sandra Nichols Found Dead (1996)

Homer (c. 850 B.C.– ?)
The Iliad (N.D.)

Hughes, Langston (1902–1967)
"Justice" (1938)

Huntington, Samuel (1927–)
American Politics: The Promise of Disharmony (1983)

J
Jong, Erica (1942–)
How to Save Your Own Life (1977)

K
Kafka, Franz (1883–1924)
The Trial (1925)

Kerr, Jean (1923–)
Mary, Mary (1963)

Koestler, Arthur (1905–1983)
Darkness at Noon (1940)

L

Lawrence, D.H. (1885–1930)
in *Sex, Literature, and Censorship* (1968)

Lee, Harper (1926–)
To Kill a Mockingbird (1960)

Levin, Meyer (1911–)
Compulsion (1956)

M

Magna Carta (1215)

Mailer, Norman (1923–)
The Executioner's Song (1990)

Melville, Herman (1819–1891)
White-Jacket (1851)
The Confidence Man (1857)
Bartleby, The Scrivener (1859)
Billy Budd (1924)

Mill, John Stuart (1806–1873)
On Liberty (1859)

N
Nagel, Thomas (1937–)
War and Massacre (2002)

The New York State Bar Association
The Lawyer's Code of Professional Responsibility (1999)

P
Packard, Edward Jr. (1951–)
Columbia Forum (1967)

Paine, Thomas (1737–1809)
The Rights of Man (1792)

Phenix, Philip H. (1915–2002)
Man and His Becoming (1964)

Pirsig, Robert M. (1928–)
Zen and the Art of Motorcycle Maintenance (1974)

Plato (? 427–347 B.C.)
The Apology (c. 404 B.C.)

Pope, Alexander (1688–1744)
The Rape of the Lock (1714)

R

Rattigan, Terence M. (1911–1977)
The Winslow Boy (1946)

Roth & Roth
Devil's Advocates: The Unnatural History of Lawyers (1989)

S

Sallust (*in full* Gaius Sallustius Crispus) (86–34 B.C.)
Conspiracy of Catiline (N.D.— c.1st century B.C.)

Schumpeter, Joseph A. (1883–1950)
Capitalism, Socialism and Democracy (1942)

Shakespeare, William (1564–1616)
The Merchant of Venice (1596)
The Life of Henry V ? (1599)
Hamlet (c. 1601)

Sherwin, Lewis (N.D.)
New York Globe

Silone, Ignazio (*pseudonym of* Secondo Tranquilli) (1900–1978)
Bread and Wine (1937)

Skinner, B.F. (1904–1980)
Walden Two (1948)

Sleeper, Ann (N.D.)
writing in Roth & Roth's
Devil's Advocates: The Unnatural History of Lawyers (1989)

Swift, Jonathan (1667–1745)
Gulliver's Travels (1726)

T
de Tocqueville, Alexis (1805–1859)
Democracy in America (1835)

Thoreau, Henry David (1817–1862)
Civil Disobedience (1849)

Train, Arthur C. (1875–1945)
The Confessions of Artemas Quibble (1911)
Mr. Tutt's Case Book (1936)
The Adventures of Ephraim Tutt (1939)

Yankee Lawyer: The Autobiography of Ephraim Tutt (1943)
Traver, Robert
(pseudonym of John D. Voelker) (1903–1991)
Anatomy of a Murder (1958)
The Jealous Mistress (1967)

Trollope, Anthony (1815–1882)
Orley Farm (1854)
The Warden (1855)
The Way We Live Now (1857)

V

Valdez, Luis (1940–)
Zoot Suit (1977)

Voltaire (*pseudonym of* Jean-Marie Arouet) (1694–1778)
Philosophical Dictionary (1764)

W

Weisband, Edward ( )
Poverty Amidst Plenty (1989)

Wharton, Edith (1862–1937)
The House of Mirth (1905)

White, James Boyd (1939–)
Hercules's Bow (N.D.)

Whitehead, Alfred North (1861–1947)
Adventure in Ideas (1933)

Winters, Yvor (1900–1968)
To a Woman on Her Defense of Her Brother Unjustly Convicted of Murder: Written after an Initial Study of the Evidence (N.D.)

Wolfe, Tom (1931–)
Bonfire of the Vanities (1987)

Wright, Richard (1908–1960)
Native Son (1940)

Z

Ziolkowski, Theodore (1932–)
The Mirror of Justice: Literary Reflections of Legal Crises (1997)

Zola, Emile (1840–1902)
"J'Accuse" (1898)

Author Index

A

Abzug, Bella, 336
Adams, Abigail (b. Smith), 68, 174
Adams, George, 65
Adams, John, 17, 333
Aeschylus, 291
Aleichem, Sholom (*pseudonym of* Solomon J. Rabinowitz), 114
Alexie, Sherman, 166
Amaniano, Tom, 283
American proverb, 330
Anonymous, 104, 157, 289, 295, 300, 329, 337
Anouilh, Jean, 83
Aristotle, 189
Auchincloss, Louis, 94, 247
Auden, W. H. (Wystan Hugh), 52
Augustine, St. (also known as Augustine of Canterbury), 181

B

Bagnall, Gary, 341
Bamberger, E. Clinton, 22, 35
Barr, Bob, 260
Barth, John, 86
Beecher, Henry Ward, 82, 152
Beecher Stowe, Harriet (Elizabeth), 184, 199, 207
Belli, Melvin M., 110
Bender, George Harrison ("Harry"), 113
Bentham, Jeremy, 64
Berger v. US, 310
Bessie, Alvah, 284
Bierce, Ambrose, 324, 328, 336
Black, Hugo, 67, 73, 146, 192, 258
Blackmun, Harry A., 119, 228
Blackstone, Sir William, 297
Blake, William, 51

Bloom, Allan, 261
Boies, David, 231, 235, 239, 240, 245
Boswell, James, 171, 182
Brecht, (Eugene) Bertolt (Friedrich), 30
Brennan, William J., Jr., 255, 269, 271
Bruce, Lenny, 334
Brussell, Eugene E., 317
Bryce, James, 42
Buckler, Carol A., 46
Burger, Warren E., 19, 112, 177, 233
Bush, George W., 179
Butler, Samuel, 25, 320

C

Caesar (*in full* Gaius Julius Caesar), 80
Caiaphas, 230
Camus, Albert, 38, 75, 198, 204, 290
Cannon, Lou, 154
Capote, Truman, 84, 90

Cardozo, Benjamin (Nathan), 140
Carver, Robert, 70
Cervantes (Saavedra), Miguel de, 81
Chesterton, G. K., 325
Choate, Rufus, 5, 180
Chomsky, Noam, 208
Cicero, 246, 260
Clark, Kenneth, 18
Clark, Tom C., 279
Cleveland, Grover, 20
Cochran, Johnnie L., Jr., 239
Cohn, Roy, 236, 332
Cole, George F., 162
Coleridge, Lord, 50
Coleridge, Samuel Taylor, 5, 127, 316
Colton, Charles Caleb, 318
Compton, Lynn, 236
Cooper, James Fenimore, 151
Cox, Archibald, 57
Crane, Frank, 62
Crombie, David, 324, 327
Cuomo, Mario, 116, 237

D

Darrow, Clarence, 23, 147, 163, 203, 302
Davis, Felton, Jr., 342
Dekker, Thomas, 329
Dershowitz, Alan M., 231, 312
Dickens, Charles, 52, 92, 106, 109, 178
Diderot, Denis, 82
Dionne, E. J., Jr, 229
Disraeli, Benjamin, 204
Dole, Elizabeth, 331
Dorfman, Ariel, 225, 309
Dostoyevsky, Fyodor, 37, 254
Douglas, William O., 22
DuBois, W. E. B. (William Edward Burghardt), 264
Dunn, Cassandra, 320

E

Ehrenreich, Barbara, 314
Eichmann, Adolf, 288
Eisenhower, Dwight D., 21
Eliot, George (*pseudonym of Mary Ann Evans*), 321

Emerson, Ralph Waldo, 30, 122, 150, 214
Emerson, Thomas I., 267
English proverb, 115
Euripides, 220

F

Fairley, Grant, 299
Faulkner, William, 58, 168, 192
Fields, W. C., 317
Fitzgerald, F. Scott, 312
Ford, Malcolm, 334
Fortas, Abe, 255, 259
Fortescue, Lord Chief Justice, 78
France, Anatole (*pseudonym of* Jacques Anatole François Thibault), 214, 230
Frankfurter, Felix, 32, 138, 186
Franklin, Benjamin, 53, 57, 149, 321, 338
Freedman, James O., 139
French, Marilyn, 37
Fuller, Thomas, 77

G

Gaddis, William, 226
Gaines, Ernest, 304
Galileo, 242
Galsworthy, John, 56
Gandhi, Mohandas K., 190, 206
Gates, Henry Louis, Jr., 195
Gay, John, 106
George, Ronald, 173
Gilbert, W. S., 339, 340
Ginsburg, Ruth Bader, 4, 169
Giraudoux, Jean, 327
Gladstone, William, 201
Glover, Jonathan, 39, 209
Gold, Ronald, 281
Goldberg, Arthur, 251
Goldman, Robert, 13, 54, 61, 93, 100, 102, 129, 141
Goldsmith, Oliver, 151
Gorden, Robert, 25
Gorky, Maxim, 74, 299
Goss, Porter J., 74
Grant, Ulysses S., 180
Griffith, D. W., 266

Grimm, Jacob, 248
Grisham, John, 128, 135, 155, 161, 164, 306

H

Hamilton, Alexander, 172
Hand, Learned, 72, 80
Harlan, John Marshall, 146, 186
Harrington, Michael, 27, 157, 160
Hawthorne, Nathaniel, 48
Hays, Arthur G., 319
Hellman, Lillian, 212
Hemingway, Ernest, 38, 127
Henry, Hubert, 298
Hesse, Hermann, 33
Higgins, George V., 110
Hitler, Adolf, 234
Holmes, Oliver Wendell, Jr., 3, 5, 7, 12, 77, 161, 272, 322
Homer, 166
Houston, Charles H., 131
Hughes, Charles Evans, 148
Hughes, Langston, 224

Humphrey, Hubert, 201, 207
Huntington, Samuel P., 18, 28, 32

I

Iacocca, lee, 107
Indiana Supreme Court, 66

J

Jackson, Andrew, 187
Jay, John, 168
Jefferson, Thomas, 4, 21, 42, 252, 333
Joan of Arc, 287
Johnson, Earl, Jr., 149
Johnson, Lyndon B., 198
Jong, Erica, 315

K

Kafka, Franz, 91, 97, 99, 133, 165, 322
Kallen, Lucille, 56
Kaufman, Irving, 107
Keats, John, 319
Kennedy, John Fitzgerald, 250

Kennedy, Robert Francis, 144, 200
Kent, James (Chancellor), 34, 87, 202
Kerby, Phil, 268
Kerr, Jean, 114, 330
King, Alan, 318
King, Martin Luther, Jr., 3, 154, 183, 185, 194, 206, 215, 218, 224
Kirkpatrick, Laird, 294
Koestler, Arthur, 307
Kristol, William, 229

L

Lamb, Charles (*pseudonym* Elia), 116
Lawrence, D. H., 263
Lee, Harper, 58, 301
Lessing, Doris, 326
Levin, Meyer, 301
Leviticus, 8
Lewis, Anthony, 276
Lincoln, Abraham, 12, 29, 64, 109, 113, 115, 123, 125

Lopez, Jennifer, 335
Luther, Martin, 241

M

MacMillan, Lord, 222
Magna Carta, 9
Mailer, Norman, 91, 302
Mandela, Nelson (Rolihlahla), 193, 213, 238, 244
Mansfield, Lord, 76
Marshall, John, 16
Marshall, Thurgood, 197
McCaffrey, Judge, 232
McCarthy, Joseph, 257
Meese, Edwin, III, 292
Mellor, David, 325
Melville, Herman, 134, 286, 294, 296
Mill, John Stuart, 19, 41, 210, 256, 259, 261, 262, 265, 290
Moore, Hoyt A., 132
More, Sir Thomas (also St. Thomas More), 47
Morgan, J. Pierpont, 108
Mueller, Christopher, 294

Murray, Patrick, 326
Murray, William (Lord Mansfield), 76

N

Nagel, Thomas, 40
The New York State Bar Association, 2, 16, 85, 108, 117, 121, 126, 130, 136, 179, 288, 291, 297
Nial's saga (Icelandic), 53
Nixon, Richard M., 36, 234
North, Roger, 104

O

Oaks, Dallin H., 177
O'Connor, Sandra Day, 145, 156, 171, 252
O'Neil, Paul, 116, 118
Osborn, John Jay, 137

P

Packard, Edward Jr., 118
Paine, Thomas, 152
Parks, Rosa, 191

Pascal, Blaise, 182
Phenix, Philip H., 10, 28, 126
Pirsig, Robert M., 70
Pitt, William, 10
Plato, 219, 243, 247
Pontius Pilate, 150, 230
Pope, Alexander, 221, 289
Powell, Adam Clayton, Jr., 153
Powell, Lewis, Jr., 8
Prosser, William Lloyd, 142

Q
Quinn, Jane Bryant, 176
Quinn, John, 287

R
Rattigan, Terence, 59
Reno, Janet, 24, 122
Roby, Pamela, 159
Rogers, Will, 332
Roosevelt, Theodore, 6
Rousseau, Jean Jacques, 6
de Rouvroy, Claude-Henri (Comte de Saint-Simon), 51

Russian proverb, 9, 124
Rutledge, Wiley Blount, Jr., 176

S
Sallust (*in full* Gaius Sallustius Crispus), 80
Sandburg, Carl, 63, 99, 343
Schicke, Richard, 280
Schmitt, Robert, 328
Schumpeter, Joseph A., 43, 262, 273
Shakespeare, William, 123, 178, 223, 308, 331, 342
Shapiro, Irving S., 68
Shaw, Lemuel, 49
Sherwin, Louis, 277
Silberman, Lawrence, 61
Silone, Ignazio (*pseudonym of* Secondo Tranquilli), 185
Skinner, B. F., 254
Sleeper, Ann, 313
Smith, Carl, 88
Stead, Christina, 46
Stewart, Potter, 67, 270, 275

Stone, Oliver, 278
Story, Joseph, 31, 79, 103, 104
Streisand, Barbra, 175
Sturgess, Judge, 153
Sullivan, Arthur, 17, 339, 340
Swift, Jonathan, 26, 44, 69, 71, 78, 323

T

Taffel, Ron, 120
Taft, William Howard, 23
Theophrastus, 20
Thomas, Clarence, 81
Thompson, E. P., 7, 14
Thompson, Hunter S., 344
Thoreau, Henry David, 104, 181, 191, 194, 205, 258
de Tocqueville, Alexis, 45, 211, 228, 253
Train, Arthur C., 103, 111, 170
Traver, Robert (*pseudonym of* John D. Voelker), 29, 60, 76, 102, 105, 306

Trevor, Claire, 120
Trollope, Anthony, 69, 85, 95, 124, 125, 242
Twain, Mark, 47

U

US Supreme Court, 268
US v. Bryan, 233

V

Valdez, Luis, 217
Vidal, Gore, 300
Voltaire (*pseudonym of* Jean-Marie Arouet), 72, 296, 316

W

Walker, Alice, 205
Warren, Earl, 11, 187, 189, 196, 203, 293
Webster, Daniel, 172
Weisband, Edward, 27
Weisberg, Anne C., 46
Wharton, Edith, 303
White, James Boyd, 89, 98

Whitehead, Alfred North, 196
Whitehead, Ted, 212
Wilde, Oscar, 11
Williams, Tennessee, 274
Wilson, (Thomas) Woodrow,
    173
Winters, Yvor, 305
Wolfe, Tom, 96
Wright, Richard, 216

Y

Yonemura, George (father of),
    184

Z

Zaccaro, John A., Jr., 232
Ziolkowski, Theodore, 223
Zola, Emile, 282